DON REVIE

Portrait of a Footballing Enigma

Andrew Mourant

MAINSTREAM
PUBLISHING

796.334092

British Library Cataloguing in Publication Data
Mourant, Andrew
    Don Revie : Portrait of a Footballing Enigma.
    1. England. Association football. Clubs. Management
    I. Title
    338.76179633463092

ISBN 1 85158 342 4

1851 583 424 1598.

Typeset in 11/13 Imprint by Bookworm Typesetting Ltd, Edinburgh
Printed in Great Britain by Billings & Sons Ltd, Worcester

Dedication

For Jenny, Anna and Tim, with my
thanks for their forbearance.

Contents

Foreword and Acknowledgments

This is a portrait, rather than the definitive biography, of one of English football's most intriguing and misunderstood figures. Don Revie's family felt unable to assist with the book. It draws on the reminiscences of people in almost every sphere of football, players, fans, administrators and management colleagues, all of whom provided valuable insights into Revie's character.

I should like to thank all the interviewees who gave me their time. In addition, I am especially grateful to Julian Barker for his researches on my behalf, and I thank also Ian Smith, Billy Simmons, John Maddocks and Jenny and Michael Thompson for their help and encouragement.

Andrew Mourant
August 1990

Chapter One

O F MATT BUSBY, the term "Ambassador" is most widely
used. Of Bill Shankly, they conjure the word "legendary".
Of Brian Clough, who boxes the ears of his own
supporters when they run on to his pitch, then kisses and makes
up afterwards before a television audience of millions, people say,
chuckling: "He's a one-off." Or something of the kind. They are
three men with great temperamental differences but the public
has been conditioned to regard them each with affection, while
considering with awe their achievements in football management.

But what do we say of Don Revie, who created arguably the
finest post-war League football club in England? That is much
more difficult. Depending on whom you ask, you will get replies
so diverse, so extreme, you would hardly think it possible each were
talking about the same subject. Ask in Leeds, where Revie carried
out his great works, and you will rarely hear a breath against him;
a knighthood, even sainthood, would hardly have been too good for
Don Revie, his most extravagant supporters may tell you. (As it was,
he had to settle for an OBE and a road named after him.)

And then turn to those players and managers who competed against him during Leeds United's great days in the 1960s and early 1970s. Some will recount their bruises, others recall his team's harrassing of referees, its gamesmanship, its time-wasting. They will recall the weakened sides Revie fielded for League matches when, having at last decided the championship was beyond him, he would make an all or nothing tilt for the FA Cup. From some opponents, you will hear scarcely a single complimentary word.

Nor indeed will you from some in the hierarchy of the Football Association after Revie's clandestine dealings that led him to abandon management of the English national side for a £340,000 contract with the United Arab Emirates. The first the world knew of this was not through the channels of officialdom but through the *Daily Mail*, from which Revie reaped further financial reward by selling his story.

Journalists made cheap little wordplays of his name. Don Revie became "Don Readies" (readies alluding to the popular slang for ready cash). Or, somewhat more sophisticatedly, it was pointed out that an anagram of his name was *envie d'or*, love of gold.

A man who had achieved so much in the domestic game, who had the total loyalty of almost every Leeds player he ever managed, who lived an exemplary family life, was on his way to collecting obituaries that would eclipse much of the good he ever did. Even when details of his will were published, a pejorative note was struck. Mr Donald Revie, OBE . . . the former Leeds United and England team manager, who signed an agreement to work tax-free for reputedly £60,000 a year in the United Arab Emirates, breaking his contract and leaving the England team in the lurch, so the media quickly claimed, died on 26 May 1989, aged 61, leaving estate in the UK valued at £67,786 gross . . ..

It was not the way he would have chosen to be remembered.

So, who was Don Revie, and what made him what he became?

He came from a poor but not quite desperate urban background the like of which seems increasingly hard to imagine. Revie was born in July 1927 in Bell Street, Middlesbrough, almost within the shadow of Ayresome Park, the home of Middlesbrough Football Club. He was the youngest of three children, with older twin sisters. The Revie family, like so many others around them, struggled to make ends meet in a time of acute unemployment. There was little to divert children – few of whose families could afford toys – save for football. In neighbourhoods such as Revie's, football provided hope

This was the Middlesbrough visited by J. B. Priestley on his *English Journey* "whose chief passions, we were always told, were for beer and football. It is a dismal town, even with beer and football." It was a town where little boys with a passion for playing soccer improvised with a tied-up bundle of rags.

Revie's father was a joiner and he was among the unemployed, spending two years out of work. His mother had to take in washing and, with his sisters Joyce and Jean, Revie used to have to collect bundles of clothes from Acklam, the most affluent area of Middlesbrough. This entailed a four-mile round trip on foot. Revie's mother used to wash all the clothes in an iron pot beneath which she had to light a fire to heat the water. Then she would scrub the clothes on an old scrubber and iron them, all for the princely sum of five shillings a basket.

There was no question of the family affording a proper football though Revie's father often kept busy replacing windows shattered by young Don's unsophisticated hoofings of this rag ball. But later, Don took pains to befriend a boy called George Tinsley, who had the most affluent parents in Bell Street. George was the owner of a real football and, as a consequence, was the most popular boy in the neighbourhood.

Revie was six when he was taken by his father to watch Middlesbrough for the first time. Afterwards, in the back streets, a bundle of rags at his feet, he would mimic the goal-scoring feats of his first player hero, George Camsell. For hours on end, he would flick a ball against a wall, latch on to the rebound and dribble round the gratings. Years later, having attained stardom with Manchester City and England, he said, as if in celebration of austerity and his unglamorous football apprenticeship, that a boy with ambitions in soccer should go out with a small ball or bundle of rags and learn ball control the hard way, for when he came to use a bigger ball he would find it much easier to control.

In 1936, at the age of nine, Revie was picked to play for Archibald School at outside-right. George Tinsley, proud owner of Bell Street's only leather football, recalls: "We could afford one because my father had the general store.

Don was promising at school. He could kick a football as hard as hell." That Christmas, he was presented with his first pair of proper football boots. Young Revie was already showing an early positional versatility, switching from the right wing to inside-left and thence to centre-forward. He played, and practised and spectated, developing his proficiency.

Tinsley remembers young Revie as "one of the lads" who could hold his own in a rough and tumble fight if the need arose. The boys of Bell Street also played an improvised form of cricket in which you got six runs if you knocked the ball over the houses. Both Tinsley and Don may have inherited their appetite for sport from their fathers, both of whom could run. "We had a 60-yard dash up the road after a street party to mark the coronation of King George VI. My father won and Don's came second," Tinsley said.

But while young Don Revie made the most of a penurious childhood, playing sport and gambling for pennies at cards, there was sadness at home. His mother had cancer. George Tinsley remembers her as "a tallish woman who suffered a lot. I can remember Don crying with the lads. We would put our arms round him and say she would get better."

All the sympathy and encouragement from his young friends could do little to assuage Revie's grief when his mother died in 1939. His days, especially the mornings, were empty and bleak, for his father and older sisters had to leave the family home early for work. These were the last circumstances in the world young Revie would have chosen for the opportunity to polish up his football technique. But as he could see no point in staying at home to mope, he left home early and, until school opened, stayed in the yard kicking his ball against the school wall. He found it helped ease the sense of loneliness and he didn't miss his mother so much.

In the streets, on a bumpy common half a mile from home, and with the teams of Archibald School, Revie developed his style. At the age of 14 he left school to become an apprentice bricklayer. War had broken out and Revie did not even consider professional football as a career. But his keenness to play the game for its own sake was as intense as ever, so he joined Newport Boys' Club with whom he played for six months before becoming involved in his first transfer deal.

The entrance into Revie's life of Mr Bill Sanderson, manager of the Middlesbrough Swifts, a well-established Teeside team, was to colour much of Revie's future thinking about soccer. Sanderson visited Newport's officials and enquired what the transfer fee would be to secure the services of Don Revie. After negotiations lasting a few minutes, a deal was struck. His move was to cost the Swifts five shillings.

At the Swifts, through Sanderson, Revie's football horizons started to broaden. He came first to understand that football was not a game for self-glorification but a team game played by eleven men who by quick inter-passing and changing of positions tried to outwit eleven other men. The collective discipline of Revie's Leeds United, in which individualistic extravagances were largely subjugated for the good of the team, were learned in part at the knee of Bill Sanderson, an engine driver who ran his team to a strict schedule. Sanderson had no time for temperamental would-be stars. He wanted triers.

On Sundays, members of the Swifts reported to Sanderson's house for tactical talks where he would dissect the previous day's match and, on a model pitch with corks representing players, point out mistakes the Swifts had made, before going on to rehearse a variety of set-piece moves. While still a player with Manchester City and before any notion of management had crystallised in his mind, Revie was extolling the good sense of Sanderson's exhaustive pre-match planning. Revie considered that the complex defensive football then in vogue threatened to paralyse all attacking ideas, so it was vital to discuss the opposition's strengths and weaknesses, and to work out a series of moves that would counter such tactics. Sanderson's discussions opened up new visions for Revie, especially the value of switching play with the long crossfield pass or the long through ball that sent two men racing through on either side of the opposing centre-half. Under Sanderson's guidance, the Middlesbrough Swifts swept all before them from 1942 to 1944.

By the Summer of '44, Revie was attracting the attention of two professional clubs: his home-town club Middlesbrough, for whom he was invited to go for trials by former left-half Billy Forest; and Leicester City whose scout George Carr had been regularly attracted by the quality of players produced by the Swifts.

With the prudence of one who had known hard times and awareness of soccer's caprice as a career, Revie's father insisted that if Don were to sign he must continue his apprenticeship as bricklayer. And so he did as, on Saturday, 26 August, Revie arrived in Leicester, wandering for hours around an alien city before reporting to the ground where, seven days after playing his final game for the Middlesbrough Swifts, he would line up on the right wing for Leicester City against Wolverhampton Wanderers.

New surroundings and new influences fed Revie's appetite not just for playing the game but for understanding all the principles of soccer in its highest form. Which often meant in its simplest form. In the mid-1950s, Revie was deploring what he felt was the worst aspect of contemporary soccer, slapdash passing, from which not even clever footballers who could beat a man on a sixpence were immune. The magisterial Leeds United sides Revie would create came to revolve around smallish midfield men with exquisite passing skills, Collins, Bremner, Giles. As soon as he had arrived at Leicester, Revie was learning at the feet of Septimus Smith, the City and England inside-forward and half-back. The strength in Smith's game was his ability to split a defence wide open with one intelligent pass.

Smith, one of five professional footballing brothers, who spent 22 years at Leicester City, remembers taking the 17-year-old Revie under his wing. "As it was during the war, we didn't have many youngsters then. But I could see he had potential when he came down for a trial and I used to coach him lots with the ball. I'd say come on with me, and we'd go into a corner and I'd teach him things" Smith said.

He drummed into the young, receptive Revie four principles: when not in position, get into position; never beat a man by dribbling if you can beat him more easily with a pass; it is not the man on the ball but the one running into position to take the pass who constitutes the danger; and the aim is to have a man spare in a passing move. Soccer would then become easy. These homilies, Revie says, were to become the broad basis of Manchester City's tactical reorganisation in 1954-55.

Smith pushed the young Revie until he dropped. At the age of 17, he was laying bricks by day, and training by night;

occasionally he collapsed in bed exhausted. Smith said: "He was an eager young player but I used to make him cry when I told him he did things wrong. He told me he would go home after the match and start to cry. I was pushing him because I believed in him. When he used to cry, I told him he should do things right. But he could cross a ball and kick a ball the right way. I would teach him the way to go . . . to pass the ball in front of the player so he could run on to it. And I would teach him how to trap it." Revie was unsentimental about his lot. He knew he had a lot to learn and that he wasn't playing football for the fun of it.

Another of Revie's Leicester City team-mates Charlie Adam, who played on the left-wing, has vivid memories of those days. "Don emulated Sep Smith. He even walked like him. He was quite a reserved lad though he had a dry sort of humour." Adam joined Leicester in 1946, after the war, having played in the same Eighth Army team as Tom Finney. He was to spend 42 years at Leicester as player and scout, only to be sacked when Jock Wallace took over as manager. "I joined up with Don. He was a nice lad, a non-drinker and non-smoker. I was the same . . . we were the only two in the team. Don was a true footballer and very popular."

He was also highly dedicated. Hour after hour, through the old-fashioned way of dribbling in and out of sticks erected six yards or so apart, Revie learned to control a ball at speed. He stuck to learning his craft, lobbing the ball, chipping it in a confined space, stroking it with the inside of his feet; a relentless emphasis on ball control and accurate passing, something to which Revie felt too few young players dedicated themselves. And it was Smith, he said, who played such an important part in shaping his career.

In the following two seasons, Revie's technique and confidence developed though, at the age of 19, he sustained an injury that might have shattered his playing future. In a home game against Tottenham Hotspur, Revie was left with a right ankle broken in three places after challenging Spurs' and Welsh international left-half Ronnie Burgess. For days Revie languished in a Leicester hospital not knowing the terrible extent of his injury; indeed, feeling he might only be suffering a bad sprain yet gradually growing more fearful as he sensed the nurses were at pains not to discuss his injury. Eventually, he was to learn at his bedside from Johnny Duncan, who in 1946 had taken over as manager of Leicester City from Tom Bromilow, that specialists believed he would never play again.

It was at this point that Duncan was to become an emphatic influence in Revie's life. In fact, doctors rated Revie's chances of full recovery at a thousand to one. But he was to draw great strength from Duncan's belief in him that he could be that one man in a thousand. It says much for Revie's fitness and determination that he was to return to a football field just 19 weeks later. Duncan's optimism had been unflagging and Septimus Smith had great faith in Revie's determination and strength of character. The unfortunate Revie also enjoyed the moral support of Duncan's niece Elsie, whom later he was to marry.

Good luck, care and courage were crucial in that come-back match. It was unsurprising that Revie took to the field in dread, wondering if he might be only half a footballer, his confidence about challenging wholeheartedly for the ball destroyed for ever. Johnny Duncan had departed him with last minute good sense: to take it easy, to get back his confidence in easy stages.

Revie survived and flourished; the recently shattered ankle held up to his normal vigorous game. He returned to the first team playing in the role of schemer, holding the ball, creating attacking moves from accurate passing. It was around Revie that Johnny Duncan had decided to create his team. In his playing days with Raith Rovers, Duncan had played alongside Alex James, who later achieved greatness with Arsenal in the 1930s, and who had been a "grafting" inside forward playing deep, spraying passes to open up defences. The deep-lying forward, connecting defence and attack, around whom the rest of the team played was, as Duncan saw it, the instrument of a successful football team.

In the 1947-48 season, the team Johnny Duncan built to this formula finished ninth in the second division. There were hopes of promotion the following season but it began instead with Leicester sinking towards the relegation zone. It was to conclude, however, with the club reaching the FA Cup final, on the way to which they disposed of Birmingham City, Preston North End, Luton Town, Brentford, and, in the semi-finals, Portsmouth, the League champions elect. The latter grand occasion was marked, not for the first time in his career, by Revie oversleeping, and on this occasion he was the cause of holding up the civic send-off for his team.

The Cup run had relied considerably on the scouting and intelligence reports of Septimus Smith, something that further reinforced in Revie's mind the importance of thorough preparation. Before the fifth round, Smith watched Preston and said: "Keep the ball away from the Preston wingers. If you do this, you will win." Leicester did so and won 2-0. Smith's intelligence, gleaned from analysing Portsmouth, intrinsically a far superior side, contained the following: "Butler, the Portsmouth goalkeeper has a habit of palming the ball over an opponent's head when he is challenged. Then he runs round him to catch the ball."

Leading 2-1, but still under intense pressure, Revie, on whom tactical advice was rarely wasted, remembered Smith's instruction to hold back in case Butler palmed the ball away from his goal thus. In the second half, as Leicester's Jack Lee challenged for a high ball, Butler did so. But when he ran round to catch the ball, Revie was there first to side-foot it into the net and poach the goal that decided the most important match of his short career.

A second serious injury was to deprive Revie of the Wembley final which he had been a major force in bringing about. In an Easter Monday League game against West Ham, Revie challenged for a loose ball in midfield and sustained a nose injury which, while bloody and painful, had not seemed sinister. Indeed, he completed another League match against Blackburn before, five days later, the nose began to bleed profusely when the Leicester team travelled to Plymouth Argyle. The nose was plugged and Revie confined to bed. But two days later, the bleeding started again. A burst blood vessel was diagnosed and specialist treatment arranged at Leicester Royal Infirmary. During the eight-hour taxi ride from Plymouth, Revie bled incessantly. Doctors at Leicester were to tell him that had he been on the road another hour, he might have died.

Revie was entitled to bemoan his wretched ill-luck. The injury denied him a Cup final appearance and a playing tour of the continent with the England squad for which he had just been picked. (There is a flavour of the superstitious bent to his character that became so marked in Revie's reflections that fate was so unkind, and also of the fickle wheel of fortune turning full circle as, six years later, he went to Wembley with Manchester City, became elected Footballer of the Year, and was picked for England.)

But Revie was too feeble even to attend the 1949 final as a spectator. He could only listen to the radio commentary in his hospital bed as Leicester were beaten by three goals to one by Wolverhampton Wanderers. Shortly afterwards, he was despatched to Ireland to recuperate during the close season. And when he returned to Filbert Street for training at the start of the 1949-50 season he found he had been made captain. But for some reason he could not quite determine, Revie detected a faint malaise about the club and felt the team spirit of the previous season had dissipated.

At the age of 22, having survived one injury that might have ended his playing career and another that could have killed him, and having reached the fringes of the England team, Revie decided the time had come to leave the club he had joined more than five years before. There was a further personal reason. In October 1949, Revie married Elsie Duncan. He recognised that in joining the manager's family his football future was complicated; that, for instance, were he to have a bad playing run yet still survive in the first team, gossips might have started to mutter about nepotism. A move was essential, as he saw it.

Players before and since have managed to live with a family connection at a club, notably Nigel Clough, who has not only survived but flourished at Nottingham Forest in the shadow of his volatile father. But he has spent all that time in a capable side, playing at the highest English level. Revie, despite his recognition by England, was with an inconsistent Second Division club. At 22, a footballer with serious ambitions had to try his luck in the First Division.

He had probably learned as much as Leicester City could offer him. Ball control, passing, tactical awareness and the importance of doing homework on other teams had been reinforced. Recognising, at his still young age, that his future at Leicester could be complicated and contaminated by possible talk of favouritism, revealed shrewdness and foresight; a managerial ability to anticipate problems. There was also much he was to take with him from Johnny Duncan's style of management, above all devotion to his players, a quality of which Revie had been a principal beneficiary.

More than 20 years later, when as manager of Leeds United Revie watched his son Duncan play football for his school, Repton, Revie Junior, joyous at having scored two goals in his house team's victory, turned to his father and asked him what he thought. Revie recalled: "I told him he had good skills, was good in the air, knocked the ball off well but was too slow. I told him I could turn a double-decker bus quicker."

In dispensing such discomfiting honesty, Revie may well have recalled the frankness Johnny Duncan had once displayed towards his own son who had aspirations of making the grade professionally, only to be told bluntly by his father that he did not have what it took to get to the top. It was an early lesson in man management, one of many that Revie was to pick up from an assortment of heroes on his own way to the top.

Chapter Two

MOVING ON was to be a protracted messy process. The first approach to Revie came from Arsenal, an opportunity one might have expected an accomplished, ambitious young footballer to leap at. But Revie found the prospect of playing for such a big club overwhelming. His mind became crammed with the negative possibilities. He might not make the grade. What would happen if he lost his form? He might be relegated to the reserves and never be heard of again. He saw London as a huge place where he would have to be a complete footballer to satisfy the demands of an imagined cosmopolitan crowd.

Not to join Arsenal was perhaps the first significant decision of Revie's footballing career based on the over-caution that would manifest itself as one of his managerial characteristics; and at the time, it was something he recognised himself. He returned to Leicester wondering whether he had made the greatest mistake of his life.

The weeks dragged unsatisfactorily on, with Revie still anxious to leave but without a deal being struck. Manchester City showed interest and Revie, now married to Elsie Duncan, travelled north-west for a meeting with City Manager Jock Thomson. But that day Manchester was sustaining its reputation as a gloomy, rainy city and the Revies had a strong sense of seeming not to fit the place.

In the end, he was to stay in the Second Division and sign for Hull City, a club without a particularly illustrious past and no obvious potential for a great future. The transfer saga had dragged on from the beginning of September to mid-November, and his signing was described at the time by one soccer journalist as a silly story that was getting tiresome. His choice of club and the manoeuvrings that accompanied it took Sep Smith, who had been used to Revie confiding in him, by surprise. "He would talk to me and ask me things about the game. But he never said a bloody word to me about the move. I thought I would have been the first he would have told," Smith says.

Revie, who had cost Leicester a £10 signing on fee from Middlesbrough Swifts, was transferred for £19,000. The real attraction for him of Hull, apart from the fact they had made a firm offer, was the opportunity of playing alongside one of his schoolboy heroes, Raich Carter.

Revie's performance earlier in the season in Leicester's home match with Hull City had caught Carter's attention. With an unsophisticated humility that many modern-day players might find quite foreign, particularly if they were on the verge of England honours, Revie had visited the Hull dressing-rooms to collect autographs. As Carter went over to sign, he made a point of telling Revie he had been impressed by what he had seen of him.

Carter, a player-manager now approaching the end of his career, saw enough in Revie's style of play to believe he might make his ideal replacement as schemer and play-maker in the Hull City team. Revie signed on a Friday night, having declared himself satisfied with the three-bedroom semi-detached house the club was providing for him, and took his place the next day in a home game at Boothferry Park against bottom-of-the-table Coventry City.

Playing alongside Carter, Revie was hungry to learn new skills and increase his tactical awareness. He admired most Carter's ability to find space on the pitch, shout for the ball and find the time to look up before parting with it; skills that would become the hallmark of one of Revie's great Leeds United inspirations, Johnny Giles. Revie had much football know-how to learn from Carter, who never cried out for possession unless he knew he was in a better position than the man with the ball. Revie was inspired by the way Carter ran things on the field and the use of the intelligent call which allowed him to find his man without stopping and looking up.

But there were early difficulties for Revie at Hull. He was still trying to play a short passing game while Carter preferred the direct through ball. With Carter playing the deep schemer that had been Revie's role, the new Hull City man found himself lying upfield, feeling out of position and out of form. But he became much happier after a switch to right-half. There Revie felt more at home and sensed he looked a better player through Carter's positional sense.

Yet overall, Carter came to view his protégé with some disappointment. "I think he let me down. I was expecting too much too soon. Revie didn't play as well as I thought he would . . . I always thought he was an inside-forward but he didn't have the punch an inside-forward should."

Indeed, Revie found it hard to settle. Carter described him as very delicate and elegant, someone who pushed the ball around with great accuracy, but not aggressive. "You have late developers. When he left here, he went to Manchester City where he blossomed." But Hull's form was inconsistent. Neil Franklin, their England centre-half and a mainstay of the side, sustained a cartilage injury. Then Raich Carter himself quit the club after a dispute with the board of directors. Revie, whose ambition remained to succeed at the highest level, was involved instead in a struggle to prevent Hull's relegation to the Northern Section of the Third Division. He was no longer enjoying his game and the high hopes he had as a youngster were rapidly disappearing. He saw no alternative but to ask for a transfer.

Carter felt he could detect other influences at work; the ambition of Revie's wife Elsie, a schoolteacher, and a keen desire to make some more money. The driving force of Elsie, whom Revie had married in October 1949, the month before he joined Hull, had also been noticed by Sep Smith. "Elsie was behind him all the time. I'm sure she was pushing him," he said.

While Revie nurtured hopes of a second chance with Arsenal, he was to be offered, and to accept, another opportunity with Manchester City, the club he had earlier rejected. This time, the decision was much swifter. Above all, Revie did not want another long-drawn-out period of waiting. In October 1951, his transfer was completed for a sum around £25,000 which included the £12,000 part exchange of city full-back Ernie Phillips.

But once again his form was to suffer, for at Manchester City, as at Hull, Revie could not immediately adopt the role and position in which he considered himself most effective. He had joined City just two weeks after they spent £25,000 on inside forward Ivor Broadis, a player who, like Raich Carter, enjoyed playing deep. Again, the Revie style was cramped by a player he described as blessed with excellent skills, electrifying bursts of speed over short distances and a fierce shot. Once more, Revie was marooned upfield, ineffective and unhappy in his role as goal-grabber. He lacked great pace, and his scheming and passing skills were wasted. As at Hull, Revie was pushed around the field again; back to right-half, then, when Broadis, who had gone on to win the first of his 14 England caps, was transferred to Newcastle United, up to inside-forward. But this time, with the option of playing deep, Revie's form improved to the extent he was picked to play for the Football League against the League of Ireland in October 1953. In that game he was given prodigious service by the Manchester United right-winger Johnny Berry, and went on to score three goals in a 9-1 victory.

But still Revie was required to cover other positions. By March 1954, he secured a place in the England "B" team that played against Scotland at Sunderland. Then a groin injury towards the end of the season put him out of the running for a full cap. Instead, to his consternation, Ivor Broadis gained the inside-right position alongside Tom Finney that Revie had coveted. He began to feel a sense of despair. At 19, he had been hailed as a future international. At nearly 27, Revie was still uncapped, still trying to find his true position, still playing in inconsistent teams.

The tactical switch that would enable Revie to realise his full potential and Manchester City to become a force in the First Division had humble, almost accidental, origins. In that 1953-54 season, Johnny Williamson, playing centre-forward for the reserves, decided one afternoon to switch his style of play by lying back behind the other four forwards. It was a method of play that threw the opposition and, by persisting with it, Manchester City reserves went on to complete their remaining 26 games without defeat. Williamson was convinced not only of the style's infallibility but that it was made to be exploited by Revie's scheming and passing skills. Revie was sceptical; he feared that in the First Division, the greater ability of players to tackle and cover would snuff it out. But its possibilities were also soaking in the mind of City manager Les McDowall who had a seemingly insatiable appetite for new tactical possibilities.

Revie and the other City players knew nothing of the ideas McDowall was pondering. In the close season, Revie was again brooding on his future, nagged by his recurrent fear of losing form through being shunted from one position to another. City had struggled the previous season but the playing staff was virtually unchanged. The prospects did not look good.

The first hint of a new approach came when City players were ordered to report for pre-season training two weeks earlier than usual. There were rigorous sessions mornings and afternoons. A further new development was that players were told they could have as much ball practice as they wanted. This new style of preparing, for which at first there was no managerial explanation, nonetheless caught the imagination of the players and there was, according to Revie, a new sense of urgency and keenness about the City camp.

Then McDowall made his grand declaration. He told the players that they were going to play proper football, keeping the ball down. Gone would be the big kicking and wild clearances from defence. The aim was for a smooth link-up from defence to attack in which the ball should do the work, and players should not waste time and energy chasing a long ball when a short and more accurate pass would be more effective.

The source of McDowall's inspiration was the Hungarian national team which had torn England apart in an international at Wembley the previous season. In particular, Hungary had made devastating use of Hidegkuti, the deep-lying centre-forward. At a more prosaic level, Manchester City reserves had flourished using a similar method. McDowall decided that Revie was to be the focal point of his remodelled team, with a brief to roam about the field as the provider and receiver of balls played to the feet.

Revie's reaction was mixed. He was excited by the scheme's innovative quality but feared being by-passed by high balls knocked over his head. Nevertheless, the team was instilled with a sense of optimism as it ran out eagerly into the August sunshine for the opening game of the 1954-55 season against Preston North End. A hundred minutes later, the City players trooped wearily off the pitch at Deepdale having been thrashed 5-0. Tom Finney and his team (it included, among others, Tommy Docherty at wing-half) had cut McDowall's new formation to ribbons. Revie himself had spent a torrid afternoon in pursuit of a ball that he never seemed quite able to reach.

It was an immediate and shattering blow. Two days later, Revie was to tell McDowall he believed the plan had no future; that teams with attacking wing-halves would cut Manchester City to ribbons. But McDowall was determined to give the scheme a month's trial. In fact the plan was swiftly and, Revie considered, fortuitously rehabilitated. Two days later again, City played Sheffield United and beat them 5-2. This time, there was a crucial tactical amendment. Ken Barnes, an attacking wing-half, was drafted in from the reserves to support Revie in the same way that Bozsik of Hungary fed Hidegkuti. Barnes proved to be an essential component. Simultaneously, the City defence was now required to be more mobile to cover Barnes whose stamina and passing skills were to prove vital to Revie's career development.

While Manchester City's flow foundered temporarily on the heavy autumn pitches, McDowall had at last created a side with sufficient cohesion to challenge for the League Championship and the FA Cup. The theory behind the reconstructed side fascinated Revie. Since the days of Bill Sanderson and Johnny Duncan he had been soaking up tactical homilies. The new Manchester City style became known as the Deep Revie plan although he was always at pains to stress it was the product of many people thinking constructively about the game. With diagrams and detailed expositions of key moves in key games, Revie dedicated 20 pages to its analysis in *Soccer's Happy Wanderer*, the footballing memoir he wrote when he was just 28. In his managerial career, he was to become greatly absorbed by detailed dossiers prepared on even the most modest of Leeds United's opponents.

The detractors of Revie's early Leeds teams with their defensive mentality might have found some irony in his near-evangelical enthusiasm for the new Manchester City. "I sincerely believe . . . the policy brought new thinking into the game," Revie said. He claimed Manchester City had forced other teams to get away from defence in depth, a negative approach by which the game had been bogged down for too long.

Once City emerged from an uncomfortable October and early November, they began tearing apart the best defences in the country because, Revie believed, oppositions were worrying from the kick-off about how to combat the unconventional deep centre-forward style. According to Revie, pure football, and first-class team work, propelled City up the League and into the Cup final. But City's exhilarating six months of success started to unravel one week before their semi-final against Sunderland, when centre-forward Johnny Hart broke a leg during a League game against Huddersfield Town. According to Revie, Hart, a "fearless forager upfront" had made the plan tick. Somewhat melodramatically, Revie described Hart's loss as like "asking Rocky Marciano to defend his world heavy-weight title with his knock-out right hand strapped behind his back".

Hart, a brave and popular player, had been plagued with injury throughout his career. He made just 169 appearances in 16 years with Manchester City and was never to regain a regular first-team place after his misfortune against Huddersfield. Meanwhile, confidence at Maine Road was contaminated by further fears about injuries. During the semi-final left-winger Roy Clarke, whose diving header was to win the match for City, was carried off with a knee injury. The club's approach to League matches became increasingly tentative. Inside-forward Bobby Johnstone, lately signed from Hibernian, pulled a thigh muscle. Revie himself had a knock on the knee and started to brood on his club's position. The scheme of things, the arrangement of the English season, the fixture pile-up, conspired against success, he felt. As a manager, it would become Revie's preoccupation towards the end of nearly every season as Leeds United, tired and debilitated through injury, became victims of their early season success.

After the 1955 season, in which Manchester City won nothing after looking possibilities for an FA Cup and League double,

Revie became convinced that unless the rules were altered so that the final would be played within three weeks of the semi-finals, no team without an unassailable lead in the League could win both Cup and League in the same season.

Manchester City lost form badly in their final League matches. These included a 6-1 home defeat by Blackpool. Revie felt it was impossible for everyone in the team to play all-out in League matches when their minds were full of a Cup final. Perhaps understandably, success through acquiring trophies, and the climate in which it might be achieved, much concerned him. While younger players in other clubs had won League Championship and FA Cup medals, Revie, who had laboured for eleven years to perfect the professional game, had none of the highest domestic honours to show for it. Then, in the 1954-55 season, he had been the focal point of a playing style that had threatened to sweep aside the rest of the First Division. At a crucial time of the season, Manchester City were to be robbed by injuries and the fearfulness that followed in their wake.

The Cup final, against Newcastle, for which Manchester City had striven so hard, was a miserable experience. They fell behind to a Jackie Milburn headed goal after just 45 seconds. Then, still early in the first half, City right-back Jimmy Meadows injured his knee and had to leave the pitch. Against the odds, City fought back and equalised two minutes before half-time with a Bobby Johnstone header. But in the second half, Newcastle's possession football ran the depleted Manchester side into the ground. City were killed off by two goals in nine minutes from Bobby Mitchell and George Hannah. For the rest of the match, Newcastle had only to keep their opponents at arm's length.

Although Revie was in favour of rejigging the football calendar to help Manchester City's cause, his view on substitutes for injured players was traditional, almost puritanical. He felt it could lead to a variety of abuses; that there would always be the temptation to bring on a fresh player merely for a man out of form. Of the loss of Johnny Hart, then Roy Clarke, then Jimmy Meadows, he believed, quite simply, that it was in the luck of the game and that luck would eventually even itself out.

If Manchester City had won nothing, Revie was finally achieving the playing success he had craved so long. He had at last been picked for England, making an inauspicious début, the first of six full caps, against Northern Ireland in Belfast in October 1954. He spent much of the match getting in the way of Stanley Matthews. But Revie and Matthews were to combine much better when they both played in the rout of Scotland the following April. There followed a rather acrimonious continental tour in May during which England drew with Spain and lost to Portugal and France. With the almost exaggerated self-restraint that Revie would show on several occasions when under pressure or being attacked, he merely suggested taking "the kind view" that some interpretations of the rules were not quite the same overseas as they were in England.

But his first taste of the Continent left him with some vivid impressions, notably the effectiveness of the calculated passing game. Revie was fascinated by the emphasis on maintaining possession in the foreign game; the passing back, sideways, frontways, any way that might frustrate the opposition. Revie's end of season call was for more artistry to be brought into the English game, and he felt that Manchester City's style could bring about a new era. Despite his late-season disappointments, Revie, whose performances had led to him being elected Footballer of the Year, felt at last he and his team had arrived. He had, so it seemed, everything to look forward to in the new season.

Chapter Three

T HE MOMENTUM that Revie's career had gathered was unexpectedly brought to a halt not by injury, nor by any twist of fate that robbed him of able-bodied colleagues but by a curious close season domestic dispute with the club. A row concerning Revie's intentions to miss pre-season training in favour of his first family holiday for six years made back page headlines. His relations with manager McDowall and the board of directors were never fully to recover and while Revie's natural footballing ability remained unimpaired, he was no longer the figure around whom things revolved as in the previous season.

At that stage in his career Revie was not a character who became embroiled in personal controversies. Yet he found himself suspended for a fortnight by McDowall before the 1955-56 season had begun and he went to the newspapers to put his case.

Revie claimed he had long informed the club and received clearance for his holiday plans from club trainer Laurie Barnett on the understanding that he reported for training a fortnight earlier than the rest of the squad. He had planned a trip to Blackpool, anxious to share a holiday not only with his wife

Elsie, who did not break up from her school teaching job until late July, but also his baby son Duncan.

Two weeks before he was due to depart, Revie reminded Barnett of his intended trip, only to be told he must see McDowall. The manager ordered Revie to commute from Blackpool each day to join the other players in training. It would, said Revie, have ruined the holiday. In the end, he went ahead and took it regardless, and according to his own account, he trained conscientiously and lost six pounds in weight.

Revie protested bitterly at this treatment. Suspension cost him two weeks pay – £27. He also made noises about seeking a transfer although he was not to leave the club for another 15 months. Yet Revie's loss of his automatic first-team place may not have been solely a reflection of McDowall's displeasure. The City manager was always keen to embrace some new system of playing and experiment with fresh players, or else redeploy his established men in different positions.

Ken Barnes, with whom Revie had developed an almost telepathic understanding on the pitch, said: "Don lost his place to Bobby Johnstone. I think McDowall thought Bobby Johnstone somehow a more competent sort of player. Yet Revie had great control for a big man and was a great player of the long ball. But McDowall thought because of his success, he could go one better. My impression was that he had to keep tinkering . . . I think we were the first to start playing with a sweeper, for instance. But by 1959 the whole side had disintegrated."

According to Barnes, Revie became disappointed and dejected although they still enjoyed a close relationship. "He was supreme as a colleague and was also very dedicated. He was a fitness fanatic and even made a point of having sherry and eggs on a Friday night because he believed it was good for him."

However, Bobby Johnstone is convinced Revie's unauthorised holiday was the principal factor. "It was the beginning of the end. I think McDowall felt he had let him down, though Don was straightforward and truthful about it. From then on, it was only a matter of time before he went. But he never said very much to me . . . he was very quiet . . . a proper gentleman."

It was apparent Revie's singular breach of club discipline had greatly irritated McDowall. "Usually, he was pretty fair," Johnstone said. "But I don't think he ever forgave Don." Yet, like Barnes, Johnstone also believed McDowall's incorrigible fascination with tactics may have contributed to Revie's partial demise. "McDowall did have some funny ideas. He tried loads of different plans. For instance, he tried to sign as many inside forwards as he could. He wanted a whole forward line of inside players. I couldn't understand it."

In the 1955-56 season Manchester City were again to perform quite well and finished fourth in the League with 46 points, the same number as they had gained in the previous season when they had been championship pretenders until losing form in the Spring. But Revie, although by no means banished, was only on the periphery rather than at the centre of things. He was to play in just half the 42 League matches. Meanwhile, City laboured their way to a second successive Cup final through a succession of tight, low-scoring games in which their margin of victory was never more than one goal. They disposed of Blackpool, Southend, Liverpool (after a replay), Everton and Tottenham on their way to the final in which their opponents were Birmingham City.

At that point, the fates, lady luck, the wheel of fortune, whatever the superstitious Revie might have chosen to call it, intervened on his behalf. Billy Spurdle, the City right winger, fell victim to an attack of boils. Bobby Johnstone had strained a calf and his fitness was in doubt. Just three hours before kick off, McDowall decided to play Revie at centre-forward and Johnstone, who described himself as only 80 per cent fit, was switched to cover for the hapless Spurdle.

Whatever McDowall thought about Revie as a club man, whatever his tactical fancies, the 1956 cup final showed that the recalcitrant deep-lying centre-forward still possessed abundant talent and match-confidence. Revie made a devastating start to the match, and was at the centre of the third-minute goal that gave City their lead. He swept a pass of more than 40 yards to the left wing, running on to Roy Clarke's return pass and flicking the ball adroitly off for Joe Hayes to score. Birmingham were to equalise before the interval but Revie was a key figure in the first of two second-half goals giving John Dyson the chance for a clear run on goal. Three minutes later Dyson and Johnstone combined to score City's third.

It was a final made memorable by the skilled promptings of Revie, a triumph of the plan that took his name yet which had

had such an ignominious start at Preston North End, and by the extraordinary courage of City's German goalkeeper Bert Trautmann who, having dived to save at the feet of Murphy, played out the last 15 minutes in agony after breaking his neck in the challenge.

Why then, a faltering career seemingly having been revived, should Revie have wanted to move? After his triumphant Wembley display, he began the following season in his favoured centre-forward position. But City's form became wildly erratic. Between mid-September and mid-October they sustained six successive League defeats in which they scored just three goals (all in a crushing 7-3 defeat at Arsenal). Again McDowall made tactical amendments and Revie was moved back to right-half as Bobby Johnstone took over the centre-forward's role once more. Revie was becoming restless. The possibility of earning money that a transfer fee would yield had also been in his mind. Ken Barnes recalls: "I remember him saying when I asked what he wanted to leave for, 'There is one thing that will tell you whether you have been a good player and that is how much you have got in the bank.' "

By November, as City's results were starting to show some improvement, Revie had signed for Sunderland who were trying to buy off the threat of relegation. He was now 29, a fully mature player, and still costly at £24,000. His departure angered some fans in Manchester who had a high regard for Revie's skills, and who sensed their accomplished team was starting to fall apart. For them, the season was indeed to prove grim. No heady excitement of a Wembley Cup run, just a defeat against Newcastle in the third round, and a slump to 18th place in the First Division.

Yet there was nothing about Sunderland's form either to excite Revie about his playing prospects. He was in a line of expensive imports bought in to help stave off a battle against relegation. The team already had players of the calibre of Len Shackleton, George Aitken, Ray Daniel and Billy Bingham. But Revie had joined a club which, to some extent, was living on its past glories, and which carried on as if the next golden age were just around the corner. Plenty of money was lavished on looking after players in the best accommodation until they found a permanent home. However, it was nearly 20 years since Sunderland had won the FA Cup. More recently, the club were fined for making illegal payments to players. Sunderland were to endure a struggle even more arduous than that of Manchester City and avoided relegation by just one place. Manager Bill Murray's desperate attempts to create a winning team failed, and he failed with them, suspended for life from any involvement in football by the FA following an inquiry into illegal payments at the club. As the management strove for improved results, they believed one way was to offer bigger bonuses – £10 instead of the maximum £4. Bill Murray left, a broken man, to be replaced by Allan Brown.

The following season was marked by disharmony and inept playing performances, and this time there was no escape from relegation. They had had a desperate struggle, tying on points with Newcastle and Portsmouth, but lost their First Division place on inferior goal average. Yet in the midst of all this Revie cut an impressive figure. His contributions are remembered by team-mate George Aitken who played at both right-half and centre-half. "He was a great player . . . he was forever trying to make the rest of the team play. Don took the game very seriously . . . and he would try to help people and give a bit of advice," Aitken says.

But inside-right Charlie Fleming is more critical. "The trouble is, there was only one way Don could play but there were ten other players on the field. We had to start off trying to get him into the game. He did a lot of things foreign to us and we could have frozen him out . . . For instance, Don would centre the ball and then disappear. He was always caught behind. I found that Don's system was alright in Manchester but everybody knew about it when he came to Sunderland, and how to play against it. Don couldn't change himself."

Fleming, Aitken and Revie became room-mates on away trips. Soon after Revie joined Sunderland, the team travelled to London for an away match. They stayed at a hotel near FA headquarters in Lancaster Gate and Fleming remembers Revie disappearing to the bedroom five minutes before the 11.00 p.m. curfew. Aitken and Fleming arrived shortly after to find their room-mate in front of his bed, kneeling down and saying his prayers. Fleming apologised for this act of intrusion on what he believed was a rite of worship. Revie took pains to make clear that it was not but added: "I say my prayers every night." "After that, we left him for 15 or 20 minutes each night to say them," Fleming recalls.

Fleming and Aitken enjoyed Revie's companionship, both at the club and away from it where they shared, among other things, a common interest in golf. Aitken and Revie also went greyhound racing. Their golfing trips often took them up to Scotland in the close season where they would play 36 holes a day, five days a week at top courses such as St Andrews or Carnoustie.

The force of Elsie Revie's personality (she was brought up in the same Scottish village, Lochgelly, as George Aitken) is vividly remembered by Fleming. "If we made a decision to do something, Don would always come back two hours later after having consulted Elsie. And if we were invited to go to a club and judge a beauty queen or whatever, my wife would stay at home but Elsie would come along to make sure he didn't drink."

Revie's cerebral qualities on the pitch did have many admirers, among them the club's assistant trainer Jackie Jones who says: "Don was a great asset. He didn't have a lot to say but I think he was reasonable . . . he was a thinker."

But the trouble was, according to Jones, that the players around him were not working together. And Allan Brown's reign was proving to be turbulent as he summarily dropped established players in an attempt to stop the rot. Yet Brown had qualities that were to make a vivid impression on Revie. After a notably wretched home performance against Everton in the relegation season, the crowd had turned on Brown and chanted for him to be sacked. But he faced their anger at the end of the match without displaying any emotion, and showing a self-control that Revie found remarkable and admirable. "I'm certain I learned a great deal from him in that unhappy moment," he said.

Forceful though his style of management was, Brown was not achieving results. George Aitken feels that relegation had not been due to the players but happened because the team was constantly being chopped and changed. "Billy Bingham, Charlie Fleming and myself were being dropped and once you were dropped, the manager had no intention of playing you again," he recalls. Jackie Jones says: "I think Brown tried to run the team with a little bit of fire but he didn't succeed. The players had too many different temperaments. He had good players sitting in the stands but was bringing in youngsters. Allan Brown was very strong-willed . . . even if the team lost seven or eight nothing, he would still play the same way."

Charlie Fleming and Brown fell out many times during the relegation season. It ended with Fleming asking for a transfer and dropping out of League football altogether when he joined Bath City. Brown's abrasive manner once led him to Fleming's bedside when the inside-right was suffering a bout of 'flu. "He wondered if I was going to play. I said I had a temperature of 103. Brown replied that he had been a commando and suggested Fleming was being feeble. I said, 'I don't care, I'm not playing.' "

Brown, Fleming recalls, expected his youngsters to play a hard-running, chasing game, rather than allowing the ball to do the work. Instead of running five yards and passing the ball 20, he got them to run 20 and pass the ball five. "And he would coach us in heading and trapping the ball . . . things that kids could do," Fleming said.

Revie was among those who fell out of favour. The team's first match of the 1958-59 season was a humble introduction to the Second Division, a home game against Lincoln. But there was no place for Revie who was banished to the reserves. As the season progressed, it soon became clear to him that his career would not be enhanced by remaining at Sunderland. In two seasons, he had played 64 games and scored 15 goals; and his cultured contribution in hard times won him many admirers. Billy Simmons, life-long Sunderland supporter and club historian, has this tribute: "He played plain, clean football and could find holes in defences. The reason why he was not a success at Roker was that the players could not keep up with his football brain."

And so by November Revie had packed his bags and was wandering, if not quite happily, once again. For a fee of £14,000 he headed once more to a struggling club but one at least that was still in the First Division. Don Revie's historic affair with Leeds United was about to begin.

Chapter Four

REVIE'S ARRIVAL brought considerable excitement to a club whose glory days had been spasmodic; one which had stumbled every so often into the limelight, but had spent its history largely unhonoured. Leeds United were neither great nor small; for a city of its stature, Leeds had produced football teams largely of modest calibre. Yet every so often flashes of ambition and individual players of talent had asserted themselves. While the team failed to win honours, one of its performers, John Charles, discovered by Leeds' Welsh scout Jack Pickard in 1948, turned in prodigious performances, first at centre-half and then as a converted centre-forward of awesome striking power during which time he achieved scoring records that may never be superceded. Under the managership of Revie's old mentor Raich Carter, who came to Elland Road in 1954, a team was constructed that could give Charles adequate support, though the virtuoso from Swansea remained the star act. When, in 1956, Leeds emerged from one of their periodic bouts in the Second Division to accompany champions Sheffield Wednesday back into the top flight, Charles scored 29 out of 80 goals. Two seasons earlier, he had scored 42 in 39 appearances.

But the upper reaches of the First Division were not in those days Leeds United's natural habitat, Charles or no Charles. Yet with him, in 1956-57, they managed eighth place during a somewhat turbulent and disrupted season in which the West stand burned down and with it were destroyed all the club's equipment and historical records. Had not nine out of the last 12 available points been squandered, Leeds United might have enjoyed the most successful season in their history.

In the midst of that poor patch, Leeds found the latest in a line of offers for John Charles's services irresistible. After having seen the Welshman perform for Wales, the president of Italian club Juventus, Signor Umberto Agnelli, persuaded Leeds to part with their provider for £65,000. Carter was given less than half that money to spend on new players, and by the end of the 1957-58 season Leeds United slumped to some 17th place. On the strength of one poor season, United's directors decided to dispense with Carter's services.

He was succeeded by trainer-coach Bill Lambton who enjoyed only the title of acting manager for seven months. In that time, he signed Don Revie. But Lambton, having been given the managership proper in December 1958, was only to last another three months. He resigned, claiming directors had interfered with his training methods. There was an unsettling period during which Arthur Turner, manager of Headington United, was approached and was favourite to take over but changed his mind at the last minute. Into the vacancy stepped Jack Taylor, a fine full-back in the 1930s with Wolverhampton Wanderers, who had spent seven unremarkable years as manager of Queen's Park Rangers.

Meanwhile, on 29 November 1958, Revie made his debut in a 3-2 home win against Newcastle United, the second in a sequence of four badly needed victories. But poor, erratic form soon struck again. Six weeks later, the captain, Irish international Wilbur Cush, stood down and, following a meeting of players, Revie was voted unanimously into the job. "I feel honoured and will give the job all I can on the field and off," he said at the time. The side spluttered on through the season yet managed to finish 15th, an improvement of two places on the previous year. But there was little optimism for the future. Public interest in Leeds United was slumping. Gates had declined steadily and from the end of January the club attracted just one League crowd above 20,000. Despite their struggle of the previous season, Leeds had attracted substantially more people to Elland Road over those latter months.

Revie was now being deployed at inside-left, inside-right and right-half. In 20 matches, he scored just two goals. The following year, he settled down at inside-right, save for a run of six matches at centre-forward as stop-gap for Alan Shackleton, the previous season's top scorer with 16 goals in 28 games. He had been bought from Burnley a month before Revie's arrival but moved on to Everton just eleven months later. John McCole was bought from Bradford City to replace him but despite scoring 22 goals in 33 games, could not stop the rot. Leeds' fragile hold on the First Division was finally to give way. The club, increasingly debt-ridden and with primitive facilities, had not given a convincing impression of belonging in the top flight. Among the notable aspects of that wretched season were that in a brittle defence – 92 goals conceded – Jack Charlton, already something of a veteran having had six years at the club, missed just one League game. It was also the season that Billy Bremner was blooded by Jack Taylor, as a right-winger. He played in eleven games and scored two goals.

Revie was already admired by Bremner as an outstanding passer and a deep thinker about the game. "What impressed me more than anything else was his vision on a football park . . . it was tremendous. And after he had struck the ball, he would pose, as if for a photograph." By chance it was Revie who first broke the news to the incredulous Bremner that he was to make his first-team debut against Chelsea. "He saw me in the car park and gave me the news. Chris Crowe was doing National Service and had to play for the army. So I played on the right wing."

The night before the match, Revie and Bremner shared a hotel room in London. It was an occasion for the senior player to show an early sign of the paternalism that would become one of his managerial hallmarks. He insisted Bremner be in bed by 10.00 pm and then, the next day, forced the young Scot to accompany him on a long walk.

Callow as he was, Bremner was shocked by the club's seemingly careless and desultory approach to crucial matches that season. "We went to play a very important game towards the end of the season at Blackburn Rovers. I remember thinking: 'I wonder where we're going to eat.' In the end, we stopped off at a cafe and had beans on toast. It was all a bit of a rush . . . nothing had been arranged. And this was the most important game of the season. We lost 3-2. Even as a young fellow, I thought 'we haven't really prepared well for this game.' "

Over two seasons, 30 players had been employed, Revie among just a handful who had appeared more or less consistently. When, in 1960, Leeds United crashed into the Second Division, there was no air of buoyant impatience for the new season, no conviction that a return to the First would be swift and successful. Revie began the 1960-61 season by surrendering the club captaincy to Freddie Goodwin, the centre-half bought from Manchester United in March, too late to hold together a beleaguered defence. Revie stepped down not because he felt unable to cope but because his superstitious nature convinced him his captaincy had been unlucky.

Another season, another division and another crop of new players; enough, in number, to make a football team. While a search for consistency had hardly been helped by the use of 24 and 23 different players in the previous two seasons, Leeds United were to use 26 in League matches on their re-entry to a lower division. Charlton, full-back Grenville Hair and Freddie Goodwin were the backbone of a defence that would remain, even in less exalted company, sufficiently uncertain to concede 83 goals. Revie's own appearances, as his thoughts turned towards management, somewhere, sometime, were becoming more spasmodic. Meanwhile, attendances at Elland Road sank gently downwards; for home matches, against unattractive opposition, 10,000 could no longer be guaranteed.

Although, in terms of results, worse was to come, the club had reached a nadir, with morale, expectations and standards of training, all low. Eric Smith, signed from Celtic in June 1960 had expected better. "The club was fifth rate and the players were undisciplined. It wasn't their fault. Jack Taylor had let the thing go. I thought beforehand I was coming to a top club. I found out otherwise in the first three or four days. We would go on long training runs and at the end, some players, quite senior players, would walk in with ice lollies in their hands."

There was, amid the general apathy, at least sufficient alarm and anger among some shareholders to force an extraordinary general meeting in December 1960 at which a disaffected minority asked for a vote of confidence to be taken in the board. In the end, after a heated debate, a resolution declaring confidence in the seven directors was carried seven to one in a poll taken of the voting shares. But the outcome was major reorganisation with the recruitment of new directors ready to invest in the club. Among them were Manny Cussins, Albert Morris and Sydney Simon. Meanwhile the voice of Harry Reynolds, a board member since 1955, was coming increasingly to the fore, although it was not until almost a year later that he would take over the chair from Sam Bolton.

The wisdom of hindsight suggests things were stirring that would give the club the basis of its revival. Reynolds, a self-made millionaire who had made a fortune as a steel stockholder after starting out in life as a railway cleaner and fireman, had a vision of making Leeds United into a great club. And despite the seemingly *ad hoc* nature of Lambton and Taylor's dealings in the transfer market, the club had already started a youth policy which showed, if nothing else did, there were signs of a management with some vision, of a view beyond the short-term. It was, of course, later to be extended and developed by Revie; indeed, by some, to be accredited wholly to him. Billy Bremner had arrived, Norman Hunter would sign in April, a month after Revie's unexpected succession, Paul Reaney would arrive in October.

Moreover, the management back-up team that was to give Revie so much vital support was already in place. Coach Syd Owen and trainer Les Cocker had been brought to Leeds United by Jack Taylor, after the club's relegation from the First Division. Owen, the former Luton Town and England centre-half, was shocked by the disarray and the apathy that he found. Cocker's and Owen's immediate task was to improve the players' physical fitness. "The first job we had was to avoid relegation. That was a desperate situation," Owen says.

Bob English, the long-serving physiotherapist who joined Leeds United in 1957 recalls; "The club was not in a good state before Don took over. There wasn't much enthusiasm, I didn't think. Jack Taylor was a nice man, don't get me wrong, but he didn't crack the whip enough. Training was slack though Don Revie, as a player, was a great fellow as far I am concerned . . . he was one of the ones that really did train. But Taylor never came out to watch people training. I think I remember him only once getting out his tracksuit and coming out to join us. But when Don took over, he was out leading them on."

Says Billy Bremner: "It just wasn't run as a professional football club. To go to see Mr Taylor: Christ, you had to go through one secretary, then another, and finally you would get to the third secretary and she would say he couldn't see you. The only time you ever saw the manager was if you travelled with the first team on a Saturday. Training was just doing laps . . . a kickabout with a ball . . . no ball on a Friday . . . just sprints."

While Revie confided his management ambitions to few people, his experience and capacity to evaluate a player was already being drawn on by Taylor who one day invited both Reynolds and Revie to travel with him to look at a player in Bolton. On that trip, Reynolds spoke of his ambitions for the club. His views on the way forward coincided in many respects with Revie's ideas about the game, and a relationship was forged between them.

As Leeds United stumbled erratically to the lower reaches of the Second Division, the directors held a meeting. Harry Reynolds then saw Jack Taylor and told him he was going to suggest to the board that it was time for him to go. Despite the fact that Taylor had another year of his three-year contract to run, he resigned on 13 March 1961. While two days earlier, Leeds United had scraped a 1-0 home win against Norwich, they had lost the previous four matches, conceding 13 goals and scoring only four.

Revie, his best playing days well behind him, was now actively considering his football future. He had already rejected an offer to go to Chester as player-coach. Then Revie became interested in the vacancy at Bournemouth and as Reynolds wrote a letter to the club describing Revie's capabilities and qualities, the thought occurred to him that he was about to sign away one of his club's most valuable assets. Reynolds came to a swift decision. He tore up the letter. Revie, he decided, should be given the chance to revive Leeds United. Four days after Jack Taylor's departure, Reynolds' protégé was confirmed as the successor.

The Revie era at Elland Road began in quite characteristic fashion with him seeking and receiving advice from people he saw as role models. For a time, Revie would also continue to play; at the age of 33 his athleticism was blunted but he still had steadying, scheming skills to offer. Reynolds, in his first talk to Revie, delivered a blunt, homespun philosophy; that success would largely mean using commonsense and having courage. For detailed practical advice, Revie, a week after his appointment, took himself off to Old Trafford for an appointment with Manchester United manager Matt Busby, whose club's charisma and achievements were Revie's inspiration. The most important instruction Revie went home with after listening to Busby's wisdom was the need to establish a consistent coaching pattern throughout the club. In that way, junior players could be promoted through the ranks to the first team and be familiar with the style of play.

Revie's appointment and subsequent success caused at least one of his former mentors some surprise. Sep Smith says: "I didn't think he would make a manager. I didn't think he was strong enough; I never thought he would be able to tell people off." But that was the Don Revie he had known as a teenager who could be reduced to tears by fatigue and harsh words. Since then, Revie had matured into an England international, married, had fathered a son Duncan and daughter Kim ; and as a player with whom age had caught up, he needed to make bold decisions about his future. His succession was not universally approved by supporters, some of whom thought the club's avowed ambition would have been proven more convincingly had an established manager with a good track record been appointed instead.

The influence of Harry Reynolds in those early days was to be crucial. His daughter, Mrs Margaret Veitch, recalls: "When he came on to the board in the 1950s, he didn't devote all that much time to the club. But when he retired in 1959, then Leeds United became more or less his hobby . . . and he wanted to make them a success. And when he was in business, my father had the attitude that everybody mattered, from the cleaners upwards to the top managers. I think he inspired Don Revie."

Revie learned quickly, and followed Reynolds' example to the letter; the concern he showed for the humblest people connected with the club became one of his celebrated management techniques. Stories of this abound. FIFA referee Jack Taylor, who probably refereed more matches involving Leeds United than any other official during the 1960s and 1970s recalls turning up at Elland Road to witness Revie giving the tea ladies a few bob to put on the horses. "If they won, they were twice as happy, if they lost, they were still happy," he recalls. Similarly, the hallowed Elland Road family atmosphere, in which players' wives were involved as much as possible with the club and sent presents of flowers on their birthday, was an extension of the Harry Reynolds management style. To Syd Owen it made sound sense. "Wives and families were part and parcel of the club. Don would do anything to be helpful to the players because he knew it would be repaid by performances on the field."

But Revie was not without some original strokes of his own. His famous decision to change the club strip from the somewhat dreary blue and gold to the all white of Real Madrid showed the touch of a man with a dream, an ideal that his debt-ridden, down-at-heel club might one day emulate the feats of one of Europe's richest and most brilliantly successful teams. The move invited astonishment among some, ridicule from others. While Revie himself felt the club had not a cat in hell's chance of reaching such heights, he was determined to try anything to get players believing in themselves. And along with the new kit, Revie decreed that on away trips, players should no longer slum it in third-rate hotels but stay in the best establishments money could buy; treatment that had come as standard at his former club Sunderland. Behind that innovation too, lay the hand of Harry Reynolds.

The first match of the Revie era took place on 18 March, a 3-1 away defeat at Portsmouth in which Jack Charlton was the scorer. Revie's home debut as manager was marked by a 2-1 defeat by Sheffield United, in a local derby for which just 13,688 fans turned up; the clearest indication he could possibly have been given of the chronic lack of interest in the team. The foreword to the programme of that match spoke of Don Revie going into the managerial side "with many carefully formulated theories on how to get the best of a team and how to groom young players for the future. That he is a practical man, he has already demonstrated with his strenuous efforts since he took over the new post."

Although he would play again the following season, Revie made no appearances in the team after January in the 1960-61 season, in which Leeds' form was always inconsistent. The only constant, alarming trend seemed to be declining gates : the last four matches of the campaign, in which Leeds were to finish 14th, all drew crowds lower than 10,000. For their final home game on 25 April against Scunthorpe, just 6,975 bothered to pay at the gate.

The following season, Revie started to try and shape the sort of side he wanted. There was a brief, false dawn – Leeds won their two opening matches – before it became clear that supporters were in for another arduous season. Albert Johannesson, who had been flown over from South Africa for trials the previous winter and made his debut in April 1961 now became established on the left wing. Billy Bremner would miss only three games, playing on the right wing or at inside-right. Willie Bell, signed the previous season from Queen's Park, would eventually become first choice at left-back. Eric Smith, playing in four different positions, missed just one game, as did Freddie Goodwin. Grenville Hair played 38 out of 42 games, mostly at right-back, Jack Charlton, 34. Gary Sprake would make his debut aged 16, airlifted to Southampton when Tommy Younger fell ill. But still Revie felt obliged to use 26 players in League matches in a desperate search for success. The forward line was his problem area. In September, John McCole returned to Bradford City and goals dried up. By the end of the season, Billy Bremner would be Revie's only forward to reach double figures – scoring just eleven.

An editorial by *Yorkshire Post* Sports Editor Richard Ulyatt in the programme for the home game against Walsall on 21 November reflected on Leeds United's ineffectual history. "For years, the club built the wrong way round. They constructed a team from the top instead of from juniors . . . far too often United have recruited with a view to plugging gaps in the first team. The whole history of the football League suggests that the teams who last longest as match-winners are home spun." But, he concluded: "I believe that Leeds United have reached the nadir of their fortunes and will shortly start on the way up."

A fortnight earlier, Revie had confessed to the fans: "We are in the throes of a financial and playing depression . . . only hard work, discipline, and clear thinking without prejudice can assist us at least to retain our present status. There is anxiety but not panic or despondency at Elland Road." The words were a preface to Revie's own view of the way forward, namely youth. Of those immature players who had yet to break into the first team, he listed Gary Sprake, "who is going to be good", Jimmy Greenhoff, Paul Reaney, then "a 17-year-old upstanding centre-half", Terry Cooper "a 17-year-old outside-left, an apprentice of great promise . . . Norman Hunter, an 18-year-old inside-forward has great ability". Revie added: "To get the best out of them, they must be brought along gradually . . . the history of football abounds with stories of clubs meeting with success when the days looked darkest. In every instance it was to be found that the people in charge were prepared to grasp success when the tide began to flow their way."

That match, against Leyton Orient, Leeds drew 0-0, before just 7,967 supporters. While there was a feeling among the staff and a few Leeds United intimates that the corner might be being turned, for most of the paying public the emergence of a brave new Leeds United was hard to envisage. "It was a race against time," says Syd Owen. "To stabilise the position, we had to get some mature professional players . . . Bobby Collins, Freddie Goodwin, Willie Bell. They were reliable honest players . . . Don knew they would help the club until we had four or five years to get the Jimmy Greenhoffs and the Norman Hunters through."

If every successful manager requires luck, then it was part of Revie's to have Syd Owen and Les Cocker among his backroom staff. Owen's principal responsibility was to develop the young players, Reaney, Greenhoff, Sprake and the rest. Owen said : "If a player has ambitions to stay in the game, he must train very hard. We were trying to develop some of these players as quickly as we possibly could. Some came to us at 15 years of age . . . then, Norman Hunter was like a bean pole."

Revie, Owen and, not least, Harry Reynolds would spare no effort in seeking to lure talented new recruits to Elland Road. "Harry Reynolds would drive down to the ground at half past three or four, after training, then we would drive up to Scotland to see the parents of a boy we were interested in. Nothing was too much trouble. Then we would drive back half way through the night and had to be down the ground again at half past eight for another morning's training," Owen recalls.

Among the first things Revie did, his memories of the skills of continental players still vivid, was to enter his emerging apprentices in tournaments abroad. Owen says: "We knew they would be extended and tested . . . that if they could perform against those kind of people, there was a great chance of them coming through in English football. Teams from Brazil would be entered in some of the competitions we played in in Europe."

The thoroughness of the new Revie/Reynolds regime knew no bounds. When Norman Hunter came down from County Durham, his mother was brought too and provided with a house. Even greater (and ultimately unsuccessful) efforts were made to secure Jim McCalliog. "He lived in the Gorbals at the time. All the McCalliog family were brought down to Leeds and his father was found a job with the Electricity Board here," says Owen.

The signing of Peter Lorimer, whom Leeds had long been trailing, illustrates Revie's determination. When Revie was tipped off that another club was all set to sign him, he and Maurice Lindley, his assistant, left by car for Scotland at 8.00 p.m. heading for Dundee. They had to reach Queensferry by 11.30 to catch the final ferry across the Firth of Forth. "Ours was the last car on," Revie recalled. "At the other side we set off again – and I was stopped for speeding as we hurtled through Perth in the middle of the night. Fortunately, the policeman was a football supporter. We arrived at Peter Lorimer's door at 2.00 a.m., knocked up the whole house and signed him. At eight o'clock our rivals turned up only to find they'd been beaten to him."

The expression that nothing was too much trouble is often repeated by Syd Owen. Revie and his management team were aware bigger clubs had more obvious prospects to offer Britain's most promising young footballers. Instead, Revie was offering pastoral care – he and his staff as father figures to help reassure wavering parents and uncertain boys that they would be looked after at Elland Road. Eddie Gray, whose brilliance was apparent to anyone who saw him, was successfully wooed to Elland Road from Glasgow and lived for a week with Syd Owen, along with reserve team player Jimmy Lumsden, before alternative accommodation was found for them.

Meanwhile, a restructuring of the board saw Harry Reynolds, already the catalyst for so much change, replace Sam Bolton as chairman in December 1961. In his valedictory notes, written in the programme for the home game against Liverpool on 23 December, Bolton spoke of the period since the war being "one of anxiety, disappointment, hard work, financial problems, staffing problems and a succession of unexpected difficulties". Bolton's retirement coincided with the appointment of two new directors, Manny Cussins and Albert Morris. But, apart from new names, Revie's hand was to be strengthened crucially by each director lending the club money so he would be able to compete in the transfer market. Harry Reynolds was coy about the amount involved. "Without going into details, I can now say Don Revie has more of the 'sinews of war' – we Yorkshiremen call it brass – at his disposal than he has had" but "how much more must remain our secret". (In fact, Reynolds put up £50,000, the other directors around £10,000 each.) Reynolds added: "I have all possible confidence in Don Revie who has shown splendid balance and unsurpassable zeal in our recent weeks of adversity."

In the winter of 1961, there was a great show of public optimism at the club – declarations that the worst days had passed. Revie busied himself looking for new players. In his search for more goals, he hired Billy McAdams, a former Manchester City team-mate, from Bolton Wanderers. One could understand Revie's high hopes: only two seasons before, he had scored 20 goals in 31 appearances for City, followed by 16 in 27 outings during his season at Bolton. But McAdams was not the solution for Leeds United, a culprit alongside other forwards of, according to one team-mate, "missing so many chances it wasn't true". McAdams appeared in only half the remaining 22 games, mainly at centre-forward, and scored just three goals. At the end of the season, Revie released him and he moved to Brentford.

Revie also gambled on another player whom many people thought had seen better days, goalkeeper Tommy Younger. Younger, who was past 30 and overweight, had been playing in Canada and was recommended to Revie by Stanley Matthews. He had also played previously for Liverpool and Stoke and won Scottish international caps. But Revie was uneasy, not least because Younger was reputed to be slack at training and a difficult temperament to handle. Moreover, two years earlier,

Younger had slipped a disc at Stoke City and been advised to stop playing. Yet he vowed to do his best for Revie, and after signing from Toronto City in September 1961, rapidly shed two stone, forcing his way into the first team at the expense of Alan Humphreys.

Younger was Leeds United's fourth goalkeeper in as many seasons. Yet the defence generally and Younger in particular were becoming a steadier unit. The previous two seasons, goals conceded were 92 and 83 respectively. Despite the struggles of 1961-62, goals against totalled 61. There were signs that at last Revie had sorted out one department of his team more or less satisfactorily.

Younger also had some advice for Revie who was still occasionally turning out for his club: the suggestion that he should give up playing and concentrate solely on management. Revie admitted the good sense of it and played his last match for Leeds, an away game against Huddersfield in March, which his struggling side lost by two goals to one. The following Saturday, Revie's team selection for the home game against Swansea had an even more resounding significance. It marked the début of Bobby Collins, the Scottish inside-forward whom Revie had bought from Everton, along with Ian Lawson, a reserve forward at Burnley, and Cliff Mason, an experienced left-back from Sheffield United, just before the transfer deadline.

Revie had been desperate to sign Collins, a combative and experienced player and now aged 31, whom Everton had seen fit to release as they rejigged their team. The Merseyside team must have seen the move as astute business, recouping the £25,000 fee they had paid for Collins after signing him from Celtic several years earlier. One of Collins' demands was that he should continue to live in Liverpool and travel over to Leeds just twice a week for training. This transfer, felt by many to be the most important factor in saving Leeds United from the Third Division and Revie from possible oblivion, began with some promise. The match against Swansea was won 2-0 and Collins, wearing the number eight shirt relinquished by his manager the previous week, scored one of the goals.

Revie had bought Collins for his experience and his fierce will to win; the first time for many years such a quality came to be associated with Leeds United. But why should he have left First

Division football for a club that looked doomed to be playing Third Division football the following season? Collin says: "It was up to me. I had had some glorious years and then I was told by Harry Catterick that I would have to fight for my place after playing like a demon. I left in anger. One day when I came back from training, Don Revie, Harry Reynolds and Manny Cussins were waiting on the doorstep. We got talking then I agreed to sign. I'd no sooner signed for Leeds than Bill Shankly rang up from Liverpool. I knew he wanted to sign me."

It was a terrific coup for Revie. Collins dismisses reports that the Goodison Park crowd had suddenly turned on him – "Harry Catterick was the only one giving me the bird." Yet his early weeks at Leeds, in which he continued to live in and do some training in Liverpool, were uneasy. Rumours grew up that he had asked for a transfer but Collins denies this was the case (though admits it did give him the chance to further secure himself financially at Elland Road).

As much as anything, Collins had been impressed by just how keen Revie had been to sign him. In the last ten matches of that harrowing season, Leeds would be easy meat just once more, in the following match at Southampton which was lost 4-1. (This was the match that marked Gary Sprake's theatrical entry into League football. Tommy Younger had been taken ill, and an aeroplane was chartered especially to fly the 16-year-old youth team goalkeeper down to the South Coast as emergency replacement.) Thereafter, Revie's defence looked to have mastered its art. In the matches, though the attack was still finding life hard going, scoring only ten goals, just four were to be conceded.

Among those matches were two against fellow strugglers Bury who by mid-April had played themselves out of trouble while Leeds were still striving for every point. It was a match that was to have a potent significance some 15 years later, for around it circled an extraordinary story: namely that Don Revie attempted to bribe Bury manager Bob Stokoe with an offer of £500 for his team to forfeit the match in Leeds's favour.

Chronologically, it was the first in a series of similar allegations made by the *Daily Mirror* in September 1977, claiming Revie had, on several occasions, tried to fix crucial matches in Leeds' favour with the offer of financial inducements to opposing players. He denied all of them, though while he initiated proceedings for libel, he never went to court to clear his name. But Stokoe has no doubts. "I remember the situation very clearly," he says. "He offered me £500 to take it easy. There were no witnesses. I said no. And when I said no, he asked me if he could approach my players. I said under no circumstances . . . and reported it to my chairman and vice-chairman."

Stokoe, an old-fashioned centre-half who had spent 14 years at Newcastle before joining Bury as player-manager, is known in the game for his honesty. He found Revie's approach peculiarly repugnant. "I was just starting out in my managerial career . . . and I was never motivated by money. Though anyone who knows Bob Stokoe will tell you he's fiercely competitive. I have a reputation for being a bad loser."

In the event, the game ended in a draw with Jack Charlton scoring a second half equaliser. Certainly, it had been no easy ride. Collins, veteran of many a hard match said: "It was a tough game . . . they were always tough games against Bury." Four days later, the two clubs met again at Elland Road in Leeds' penultimate fixture. The programme notes have a polite, ingenuous flavour under the circumstances. "Bury are home and dry after a splendid rally in the last few weeks – and this before they began their Easter task which consisted of home games against ourselves and Huddersfield Town and today's match . . . The hope of United's supporters is that this time, Mr Stokoe and Mr Revie will both have achieved their objective in the same season."

Stokoe recalls: "After that match, I lost all respect for Revie. On that Tuesday night we went to Leeds, Revie never spoke. But I had one of the finest games of my life. We drew 0-0." In such harrowing times, public interest in Leeds was reviving; 21,482 turned up for the match. But United's ordeal was not yet over. They were still not safe and had, as their final fixture, an unpromising away fixture at Newcastle United from which they needed to secure a point. But playing in a stiff wind and on an unyielding pitch, Revie's team struck rare form. Bobby Collins, Willie Bell, playing out of position as an inside forward, and Albert Johannesson were key figures in a performance of collective discipline. Johannesson's first half goal on 37 minutes, a header from Johannesson's cross by McAdams after 65 minutes and an own goal by Newcastle right-back Bobby Keith ten minutes later, gave Revie deliverance and occasion for a tearful celebratory embrace of his chairman and mentor, Harry Reynolds.

Chapter Five

THE FINALE to the fraught 1961-62 season showed that there was the basis for recovery. Attendances at Elland Road had improved on the previous year when the season had been merely mediocre, without the spice of the fight for survival. Revie, with the guarantee of directors' cash behind him, waded into the transfer market once more. He bought Jim Storrie, a hustling inside-forward from Airdrie who would, as the season progressed, be converted to centre-forward. And, with a flourish of atypical managerial flamboyance, Revie brought back John Charles from Juventus for a club record fee of £53,000.

It was a gesture of high ambition, in the spirit of his ceremonial adoption of the colours of Real Madrid one year earlier. The first game of the season, away at Stoke, attracted a gate of 27,118 and brought a 1-0 victory, courtesy of a goal by Jim Storrie. The media interest in Charles was intense, for his goals and powerful play had helped put Juventus among Europe's footballing élite. But it became clear rapidly that the continental game had left Charles ill-equipped for the hard-running English style. Moreover, he treated some training sessions with a levity that riled Les Cocker. Charles's return to the ground where he had been a legend, and continued to be long after his second departure, lasted just eleven matches in which he scored three goals. But at least Revie was not to suffer financial embarrassment. In November, Charles was on his way back to Italy, this time to Roma, for a fee of £65,000.

His other recruit, Jim Storrie, was scoring more consistently and suddenly looking a bargain at £15,000. His signature was another triumph for Revie's persistence for, when Revie had approached him the previous season, Storrie had not fancied his prospects at the struggling Second Division club. But on the second visit, Storrie found Revie's expressions of high ambition hard to resist. Whether it was an apprentice or a seasoned professional, Revie had a habit of getting his man.

Neither would he give up when difficulties arose. Gary Sprake had come up to Leeds as a young apprentice to play in a trial game but was soon on his way back to South Wales, homesick and convinced he had performed badly. "But Revie came down to Swansea to pick me up. He said I had talent and thought I was good enough," Sprake says.

In the 1962-63 season, Sprake and a batch of other youngsters who had been trained rigorously by Les Cocker and Syd Owen were to be given their first team opportunity by Revie as, once again, the club ran into poor form. Following a home defeat by Bury on 5 September, Revie drafted in four of his hungry young men for the away game at Swansea three days later. Afterwards he admitted that the failure of the Charles venture had forced him to bring them into senior football sooner than he would have liked. He was haunted by a fear that they were unready and could be spoiled by the strenuous demands of the Second Division.

Their number included Sprake, Paul Reaney, Norman Hunter and Rod Johnson, who scored in his début to help secure a 2-0 victory. It was a game in which Revie felt Leeds played their finest football of that season. Yet it was not Johnson but the other three raw young débutants who were to make the positions of goalkeeper, right-back and left-half their own, not only that season but for years to come. Hunter, a raw, gangling lad of 18, did not miss another game and Reaney, still 17, was absent only for the 6-1 home win over Plymouth on 17 November.

With long-serving defender Grenville Hair now at left-back, Willie Bell at right-half and Jack Charlton commanding the centre-half position, the backbone of a new Leeds United was starting to emerge. Meanwhile goals, at last, were coming regularly; from Storrie, Johanesson, Lawson, Weston, Bremner – from all sides; 55 were scored in home matches alone, five more than for all games in the previous season. The success of the new recruits said much for Revie's training methods. Syd Owen in particular, had been urging them on, quick to spot capabilities that might have escaped many people outside the professional game. "Reaney . . . he wouldn't catch the eye . . . but you knew he would do things efficiently every time he went on the field," Owen says. That Jack Taylor had brought some of the talented youngsters into the club is not infrequently dismissed. Johnny Giles, who would join Leeds the following season, says: "It is because of Don and the environment he created at Leeds United that he produced Paul Madeley, Paul Reaney and Norman Hunter. None of those lads were naturally gifted players. They worked very hard at their game. Norman wasn't so strong . . . wasn't a good header of the ball. If they had been at other clubs, they might not have been good players at all."

In fact, Hunter had nearly been allowed to slip away. As an apprentice, he had been about to sign professionally when Revie's predecessor, Jack Taylor, had had second thoughts. Hunter remembers: "He said hang on a few months. In the meantime, he got the sack. I was Don's second signing."

More established players were also causing Revie difficulties, especially Jack Charlton who, for a long time, had fixed ideas about his role as centre-half. Revie, among other things, had ordered him to stick to the opposing centre-forward when opposition attacks came into the Leeds half. He was to have a series of arguments with Charlton over the latter's eccentric positional play early that season which was costing the Leeds defence goals. Another row followed Charlton's erratic display during a 2-2 draw at Luton in September. This time, Revie imposed his will on Charlton. Playing to new instructions brought the belated rise of Charlton to a centre-half of international stature. Norman Hunter recalls : "Don was having a lot of problems with big Jack . . . he doesn't like being told what to do. But the gaffer sorted him out . . . though Jack never likes to this day anyone telling him what to do. He had problems with discipline with himself. The big man needed guiding . . . he needed someone to get hold of him." Charlton admits he did not enjoy training and the sound of Syd Owen shouting home truths at him. When they were both players, Revie had accused Charlton of having a chip on his shoulder, of spoiling things for other players with his recalcitrant attitude. For the first difficult year of Revie's management, their relations were fraught and Charlton's principal ambition had been to get away from Leeds.

As, for some time, had been Billy Bremner's. Ever since joining the club in December 1959 as a 17-year-old, Bremner had been homesick. Jack Taylor had allowed him to go home to Scotland some weekends but Bremner remained restless and dissatisfied. Neither was he easily swayed by Revie, at first. But Revie had his own methods. The source of the problem was Bremner pining for his girlfriend (later to be his wife) Vicky. Bremner recalls : "The gaffer went up to Stirling to speak to her parents. I couldn't believe it . . . he was saying maybe it would be better if Vicky came down to England, which is really something he should never have done."

Bremner did not realise it at the time but Hibernian were desperately keen to secure his services. "Later, I got to know they came in for me at £30,000 . . . it was a colossal amount of money then. Little did the Hibs manager know the gaffer had made up his mind I wasn't going. Don would want £35,000, then £40,000. Then I gradually settled down and started playing well, although I was on and off the transfer list."

Revie was quite desperate not to lose Bremner. He had already fended off a bid from Everton, who were prepared to pay £25,000. The offer had been a considerable temptation to the Leeds United directors, ever mindful of the club's crippling £250,000 debts. When Revie realised the offer was under serious consideration, he threatened to quit. Bremner recalls: "He said, 'If he goes, I go, because I want to build a team around him.' Then he walked out of the boardroom down to Les Cocker and said, 'Les, let's pack our bags.' But Harry Reynolds came down the stairs and said, 'Don, forget it, lad. Billy's going to stay . . . you can stay.' "

Revie and his fiery protégé had a number of tiffs. Bremner says: "We had a hell of a dust-up because he wanted me to play wide, on the right. I said I wouldn't . . . I was going to play in a central position. He said I wasn't ready for that yet. I had been ready a year ago in the First Division. Eventually he said:' You'll play where I bloody well tell you.' "

As Bremner dropped into the reserves, he remained unsettled, with Revie making monthly entreaties for him to come off the list. As Bremner was eventually moved into central midfield, Revie continued to persuade. The emerging talents of Hunter and Sprake gave Bremner some cause for optimism. "The gaffer said that the team was developing . . . we were going to be successful. He convinced me and I took my name off," Bremner says.

It was to be a strange season, dislocated by the big freeze of 1962-63. From 22 December, a 2-1 home defeat by Sunderland, until 2 March, Leeds were without a game. Just before the bitter winter set in, Revie added to his ranks inside-forward Don Weston who marked his début with a hat-trick in a 3-1 victory over Stoke City. When, after their enforced lay-off, Leeds were plunged into an intensive run of games, they struck excellent form, winning six and losing only two of their nine games in April; and scoring 19 goals in the process. Over their last five matches, the team lost consistency but there was sufficient evidence to suggest Revie's side of youth and experience had cause for optimism.

Revie was still in the market for more players to do the job he wanted. In the close season, Johnny Giles, the young Manchester United inside-forward who, that season, had won a Cup final medal, became available. Still only 23, Giles had joined the Manchester club as a 15-year-old. It seemed strange for him to be anxious to move from one of England's most glamorous clubs which, once again, had started winning trophies. As it happened, Giles still felt something of an outsider, despite having been a first-team regular that year. Matt Busby had made several big money signings but Giles had become demoralised by a lack of team spirit and constant bickering among his ill-suited colleagues. "I played in 38 games and all the Cup matches. But I'd been there as a young boy and maybe not appreciated as much as I should have been. And Leeds had had a good run the previous year. When you are in the game, you notice these things. There was a feeling about them. But Don was a big factor . . . he was a great football man. I would have much preferred to join an up and coming Second Division team than a poor First Division one. They had also signed Bobby Collins a year or two back. That was a big factor too. From the time I joined, Leeds were successful. Don had learned from his playing days all the faults of managers. He knew what he wanted to do . . . he was a very ambitious man, a very driven man." Alongside Collins, Giles was to be one of Revie's most inspired buys. It would become hard to believe that a criticism of Manchester United's supporters was that his game had lacked bite, a bit of devil.

Revie's Leeds United side began the 1963-64 season with the serious single-minded purpose of escaping from the Second Division. While goals were being scored with less abandon than the previous campaign, points were being ground out with greater consistency. Frequently, it was not to make for pretty viewing. As Leeds United's success started to attract attention, so did the style of play, a style that euphemistically might be called uncompromising. But, as Norman Hunter put it "We had to get out of the Second Division. We were a physical side, yet we had a tendency that we could have gone and beaten sides better than we did . . . we would have battles on our hands against teams we had outplayed."

Early that season, Revie had been infuriated when Leeds, already leading the table, attempted an unnaturally aesthetic style of play during a home match with Derby County. Finding his team 2-0 down at half time, Revie raved at his players and ordered them to revert to their hustling style. Acting under orders, they eventually levelled the score and salvaged a point.

Giles had some misgiving about the side early in the season, feeling it was still naïve, long on effort but short on guile. After his first match, a 3-0 home victory over Bury, Giles considered Revie's and Reynolds's ambitions for the club wildly fanciful. But as the season progressed, the last thing Revie's Leeds could be accused of was innocence. It was curious that Revie, who professed high soccer ideals, and whose play had been characterised with cerebral elegance, should have bred a side that was to employ every tactic in the rule book, and several outside it, in its unswerving quest to gain advantage. Foul play and various strains of gamesmanship became synonymous with the club. But the players who were to benefit from the results obtained under Revie's new regime are sometimes coy about their recollection. Norman Hunter admits players used to go down and exaggerate injuries to interrupt the flow of the other team or to pass on messages. "Yes," he says, "that was a bit before its time though people do it now . . . and when we took the ball to the corner flag (to waste time) . . . that was gamesmanship. A large percentage of that was Don's thinking." On the feigning of injury that would upset so many opponents, Bob English responds, as if by way of justification . "How often do you see that today . . . people diving? As far as I am concerned, we played it hard but fair." Johnny Giles says: "Don might have gone overboard but without that, we wouldn't have got anywhere."

Revie's team became involved in some notably ferocious matches that season in its myopic drive for results. In a draw with Preston at Elland Road in November, referee Eric Jennings halted play and lectured both teams about their behaviour. The two games against rival promotion challengers Sunderland at Christmas were characterised by acrimony, violent tackling, and exchanges of insults. Johnny Giles considers his young team was particularly susceptible to provocation and that it took a long time for them to master greater self-control.

But the points were coming, the fans returning. The home draw against Sunderland on Boxing Day drew 41,167 to Elland Road. The fixture against Manchester City on 11 January (a 1-0 victory) drew 33,737; the local derby against Huddersfield on 22 February (a draw), 36,439; and this despite being a patch of indifferent form. Some of the hot-headed matches had taken a toll on players; Jim Storrie played only two more games that season after being carried off with a leg injury during the rancorous 2-0 defeat at Sunderland on 28 December; Jack Charlton lost a third of the season after injury in the home match against Charlton Athletic in November; and the third round FA Cup tie at Cardiff City saw Freddie Goodwin break his right leg in a clash with ex team-mate John Charles. Revie used this opportunity to blood young Paul Madeley at centre-half, but unlike Sprake, Reaney and Hunter, he had not yet arrived to stay. Madeley would play just four games in the number five shirt that year and in the next only half a dozen, in assorted defensive positions.

In the latter stages of winter, goal-scoring once more became a problem. Ian Lawson was out of favour with the fans and out of form. Revie was driven into his boldest transfer since buying John Charles as, in February, he paid £55,000 to Middlesbrough for centre-forward Alan Peacock, a robust attacker and a powerful header of the ball who had won international honours with England. Peacock did not make a dramatic impact but settled in gradually to score crucial goals as the season entered its tight, tense final phase.

Towards the end of that season Revie's love of methodology and elaborate planning found its most celebrated expression. It happened as a result of him asking Syd Owen to look at and report on a young player in whom the club was interested. Owen, dutiful and thorough to the last, filed an account so exhaustive that it brought delight to Revie's heart. "It was a masterpiece," he declared, and it marked the birth of the famous Revie dossiers, the sometimes excruciatingly detailed appraisals of opposing players that Leeds United players were required to digest before doing battle on the field.

Mention of the dossiers he initiated makes Syd Owen laugh a little nervously, as if faintly embarrassed by the subsequent notoriety that became attached to them. "I would write them out in long hand and they would get typed out for Don's benefit. We felt that by doing that, we were furnishing the players with all the information we possibly could." But did it lead to over caution? "Yes," Owen says, "it probably did. I am the first to admit this." Norman Hunter agrees. "I think we did pay the opposition too much respect. But whatever Don did at that time, you had respect for. Though looking back, I would never have a dossier to play against a team. I would have certain points. We analysed teams far too much."

Revie was never to abandon the dossiers, not even when his fully mature side was playing brilliant irrepressible football at the top of the First Division. "They didn't go out of the window," Hunter says. "One thing Don never did was to change his routine. It went on up until the time he left. That was his way . . . and sometimes, even though you were thirty-odd, you were sitting there through half an hour, three quarters of an hour, talking about players you already knew. But that was his way."

Billy Bremner considered the dossiers were a ritual to be endured. "I'd look at the dossier though I wasn't taking a lot in. But I thought I'd better pay attention because if he said to me, "What was I saying there?' and I wasn't paying attention, he wouldn't be too pleased. Yet if we played Arsenal on the Saturday and then again on a Tuesday, three days later, we'd have the same dossier. The only time I would listen was when he was talking about continental players I didn't know."

The dossiers made Peter Lorimer doubt if Revie had true belief in his team. "We used to play some teams at Elland Road that weren't even entitled to be on the same pitch as us . . . in the cup and suchlike. He was so thorough that at the end you were creating a bit of respect for a team you didn't have to . . . a little bit of fear. He wanted you to be totally aware of things other teams did. You would go through the same talk as you probably had the year before. We knew how we were going to play anyway."

Revie's way with young players was something that also didn't change. Of all the youthful talents he was to recruit to Elland Road, Eddie Gray, spotted as a left-winger playing for Glasgow schoolboys, had the most extravagant, eye-catching ability. He was also greatly sought after. On first seeing him play in a representative game against England at Nottingham Forest, Syd Owen recalls: "I could hardly believe what I saw . . . the boy had so much talent. We went up to Scotland many times to persuade him to join us." But the competition was intense.

Jimmy Lumsden, who was also playing for Glasgow schoolboys and who was brought down to Leeds by Revie at the same time recalls : "Every time I went up to Eddie's house, somebody was there from some big English club . . . and Celtic were there every night. Arsenal were flying him down to London. But he picked Leeds. Everything boiled down to the manager. He convinced everybody they were going to go places.

"I remember the day Don Revie took us down to Leeds. We had our bags packed. Don went to Eddie's school and the two of them went off to see the headmaster. The cases were already in Don's car. They went off to ask if Eddie could leave school there and then. I think they were glad to get rid of Eddie because he wasn't any good at school anyway!"

"Don Revie's great love was the Scottish lads . . . he liked their attitude. Bobby Collins was the general . . . as soon as he moved out on to the park, he was the boss for Revie. He had the respect of everybody. Collins was a winner . . . everything was for real on the training park."

Revie, who often cut such a diffident and inhibited image in public, was quite capable of striking fear into the hearts of his players. Wing-half Lumsden, who spent six years at Elland Road, almost entirely in the reserves – patiently waiting for the odd first team opportunity created either by injury or by Revie's grand design to field a weaker team for an unimportant match, says: "He was a hard, hard man. His family had struggled years and years ago and I think he thought 'That will never happen to me.' There was just something about the man. If you did wrong, he would nail it right away. One of the younger lads had misbehaved when his landlady was away and he was in digs on his own. Don sacked the boy. He had had a warning, and if you had been warned before, that was it."

And despite Revie's emphasis on intimacy and the family atmosphere, there were, Lumsden recalls, instances when players preferred not to go to him with their problems but would instead seek out Maurice Lindley, the affable assistant manager. "You were a bit scared of Revie. If he just walked in the corridor and you were on the ground staff, your immediate reaction was to jump," says Lumsden.

"There were other little things; first team players out for a drink when they shouldn't have been, though I wouldn't say they were drunk. Don Revie would take a player in, nail him, and that would be the end of it. He was frightening. And he would also get angry if he told you a certain thing about a player before you went out on the pitch, and then that player beat you by what Don had told you. He would get mad and would thump the dressing-room table. All the homework he and his coaches had done would have been wasted."

Yet Revie was, for Lumsden, everything a manager should be. As well as knowing the game inside out, he had a sure touch when players were distressed. Lumsden recalls: "When my father died, he was fantastic. He took me into the office and spoke to me for about an hour . . . told me to take as much time off work as I wanted. He sent flowers to my mother and then got her down for a week and paid for it. He didn't have to do it but that's how he created this spirit. He looked after people."

Revie took care of his lesser lights financially, too. Patient though Lumsden was, there were times when he wondered if ever he had a future at Elland Road. "I went in to see Don Revie a couple of times about it. I think he respected me for that. He told me to sit tight. He didn't think I would be any use to another team just then. He was trying to give me advice. It was a nightmare trying to break into the team. The likes of Paul Madeley weren't even guaranteed a place. But Don kept everybody happy with bonuses. He was strong with the directors: he would make the point that if he wanted 16 or 17 players to be happy, he would have to pay them in bonuses. I can remember coming back from a reserve game at Everton. We had been beaten but he was in a good mood. He put his arm around me and said: 'Come in and see me on Monday . . . we're putting you on half bonuses.' "

While, according to Jimmy Lumsden, Revie was not a man of a thousand rules, those he imposed were sacrosanct. One of those was punctuality, something that had not always been Revie's strong suit as a player. After Leeds United had regained the First Division and started to conquer Europe, Lumsden recalls a return flight from Budapest to Manchester in which Revie ordered everyone straight on to the team bus. "There was one director who was late, trying to bring, I think, about 30 bottles of wine through. As soon as he walked on the bus, Revie said: 'For that, you give every lad here a bottle of wine.' And he did. I've seen directors who haven't been on the team bus, and he's left."

As the 1963-64 season reached its latter stages, winning form returned to Leeds United. Alan Peacock was making his mark, the goals that had been so desperately lacking, started, if not exactly to flow, to arrive when they were most badly needed. When they won 3-0 at home against Southampton on 7 March, it was the first time the club had scored more than two goals in a match since 26 October, when they beat the same club 4-1 at The Dell. Now Leeds embarked on a steady, assured run-in. The March win over Southampton was the first of four successive victories culminating in a 1-0 defeat of Newcastle United which drew a Good Friday crowd of 55,038 to St James' Park. The match, played on an extremely windy day, was settled by a freakish goal from Johnny Giles when an intended centre was caught by the breeze and curled into the Newcastle net.

Thirteen years later, the attention of the *Daily Mirror* team investigating Revie's alleged attempts to fix matches was drawn to this game. Its "evidence" was, to say the least, tenuous. The *Mirror* story claimed that Revie, his team stricken by injury, had telephoned Stan Anderson, a former team-mate at Sunderland and now captain of Newcastle, and asked him if he would offer the Newcastle players £10 each to throw the game. The telephone call, or at least Anderson's half of it, was said to have been witnessed by an unnamed reporter visiting Anderson's home. The *Mirror*'s source claimed Anderson had reacted furiously, slamming down the telephone on the Leeds manager. Close examination of the *Mirror* report yields few hard facts and certainly no confirmation attributable to Anderson that the exchange had occurred.

Anderson, who had liked Revie and been one of his room-mates when Sunderland travelled to away matches, says: "The stories were a tissue of lies. The press were gunning for him at the time. I denied it from the start – it was all innuendo – and I deny it now. I went to see my solicitors about it but they said the story hadn't said anything about me. The whole thing was based on a telephone call that never took place."

The return home game against Newcastle on Easter Monday brought Revie's team a 2-1 victory, a crowd of more than 40,000 and a dazzling individual goal by Albert Johannesson. Promotion for Revie's reconstructed team was just two matches away. It came in the away game at Swansea on 14 April where, by half time, two goals from Alan Peacock and one from Johnny Giles clinched matters. But Revie, almost pathologically superstitious, did not buy the champagne they were to drink beforehand, fearing it might tempt some malign fate. Instead, he and several players made a tour of the Swansea pubs after the match in search of celebratory bottles. It did not take them too long to become inebriated on the train journey home.

Although the principal objective had been achieved, the Leeds players still had some hunger; they were anxious to finish above Sunderland whose football had been lauded more often than their own. The Second Division title came at Charlton on 25 April when Alan Peacock scored both goals in Leeds' 2-0 win. Revie's team had suffered just three away defeats all season and won 12 times; a triumph, if it can be called that, for its method of stealing goals then shutting out the opposition by defence in depth. Often it had not been pretty. For sure, the

Second Division had never seen the likes of Revie's men and boys before. A pattern of play, a will to win regardless, had been instilled in his team; one that would not wilt easily in the face of whatever skill and refinement might await them in the First Division.

Chapter Six

THE MOMENTUM that had propelled Revie's Leeds into the First Division appeared to stay with them as the season opened. No one but the most adventurous optimist would have put money on the team winning its first three fixtures: away to Aston Villa (2-1), home to Liverpool (4-2), then at home to Wolves (3-2, after being 2-1 down at half time). For Johnny Giles, that opening salvo was crucial: it gave them confidence when a poor start might have disheartened a side of which only a handful had previous experience of top grade football; and the points provided a cushion against a somewhat lean run that followed immediately.

Jim Storrie recalls how Revie's ambition and enthusiasm infected the players. "After winning promotion, most managers would talk in terms of consolidation. He spoke in terms of finishing in the top four. He said, 'We will come up against some world class players but we will be the best team in the League.' So he had the optimists among the lads thinking we would win the League and even the pessimists thought we might finish halfway up."

Alan Peacock had been injured from the start and Willie Bell picked up an injury after the fifth match of the season. Revie's response was to draft in the promising young Terry Cooper, originally brought to the club as a left-winger (where he had played in two games at the end of the promotion season), to left-back. But Cooper was not yet to make the position his own. Revie immediately reinstated Bell once he returned to fitness; and Cooper, despite his manifest talents, would have to wait another three seasons before replacing him.

Revie's men arrived in the First Division super-fit to help compensate for any possible technical deficiencies. Meanwhile, their "total commitment" of the previous season brought them early notoriety. A Football Association report made public the fact that Leeds players had earned more referees' cautions – 18 – in the previous season than any other League team. They were labelled the roughest side in the country. Aggrieved that the figures had been let out of the bag, Leeds directors wrote to the FA to protest. A line of their missive had a curious flavour; disquiet with an undertone almost of menace – "It could lead to some very unsavoury incidents . . ."

Most of Revie's great players deny there was ever any deliberate intention of 'clogging' an opponent. Billy Bremner, who made several visits to appear before FA disciplinary hearings said: "I've never known the gaffer say to us go out and kick them, or waste time. But I would say critics of that early side were justified. We were young, we were cocky, and we weren't the most attractive team to watch. When we were away from home and we scored a goal, I can remember thinking that the 25,000 people or so watching would be as well going home there and then. When we came out of the Second Division, we were always winning 1-0 but we could see we weren't contributing a lot to the general entertainment. I could understand people thinking it wasn't nice to watch. And the managers thought we were bloody winning too much!"

Peter Lorimer claims a press sympathetic to the established London clubs exaggerated matters. "Leeds' record for sendings off was no worse than other clubs," he says. "Chelsea had a very hard side, Everton, Liverpool. That's the way the game was played then. Don never told us to rough it up. He knew he had players who liked to play it that way . . . Norman Hunter and Paul Reaney."

Later, Bremner admits, Leeds United were to learn some of the finer arts in gamesmanship from their European sorties. "We thought a lot about our game and picked up traits from the Continentals. What we called cynical in this country was called professional when the Italians played it. We picked it up from them . . . how they would just walk out to take a corner, or if the game was getting a bit heated, someone would feign an injury. Things like that."

Bremner's temperament was at the centre of some of the early problems. "He was being pilloried by opposing players off the ball, elbowed, that sort of thing," Storrie says. "Then when he reacted, everybody saw it. He was spending more time sitting in the stand, serving out suspensions, than on the pitch."

Revie, Storrie says, responded by calling a council of war. He gathered together his players and told them that everyone in the team should look after each other, that no-one should get isolated. Should Bremner be picked on, he was to walk away and the rest of the players would draw the matter to the referee's attention. "If any one of us were singled out, we were all to respond," Storrie says, though he denies Revie was explicitly laying down a policy of an eye for an eye. But left to highly motivated young men who could barely wait to get inside a Leeds United shirt, it was clear Revie's dictum meant they were to take nothing lying down. And referees who failed to spot transgressions against Leeds players could always rely on their unofficial assistance.

The season was less than two months old, and Leeds United about to run into their richest vein of form yet, when, on 16 October, a newspaper story leaked out that Revie was preparing to abandon Elland Road for the managerial vacancy at Sunderland. In May 1963, Revie had signed a contract due to keep him at Elland Road for another three years but as the side had grown successful beyond most people's dreams, he became consumed with a strong sense of being under-paid and under-valued. The following day there was, for its time, a vociferous and impassioned demonstration of Leeds supporters after the 3-1 home defeat of Tottenham. That evening Harry Reynolds was injured in a car crash returning from another match in Yorkshire. Revie was among the first of his hospital visitors. While the Leeds manager was later to be saddled with a reputation for greed, Reynolds' daughter, Mrs Margaret Veitch recalls him saying: "It's not about the money." As much as anything, Revie appeared to crave recognition. From his bedside, Reynolds, who favoured Revie winning an improvement in his terms and conditions, was pleased to hear of the volatile scenes at Elland Road. These would, he felt, help sway board members who possibly valued their manager less highly than he did. In the end, Revie's claim for better rewards was met. To one journalist, Revie told a rather mawkish story of his heart being melted and his mind changed by a group of apprentices in tears at the prospect of his departure as he made what he intended to be a final visit to Elland Road to collect his kit.

Three weeks later, Revie's side was embroiled in controversy once more. The occasion was a fixture at Everton. A foul on Jack Charlton in the first minute set the pattern for a spiteful, ferocious match in which Everton full-back Sandy Brown was sent off after just five minutes for fouling Johnny Giles. The home crowd became increasingly venomous when Willie Bell headed Leeds into the lead ten minutes later. After 35 minutes, Bell and Temple collided on the touch line. Amid the furore that ensued, referee Roger Stokes created history by taking both teams off the field in an attempt to restore the rule of law. Storrie recalls: "He came into each team's dressing-room and said that if we didn't stop kicking each other and start playing football, he would report us to the FA."

For Bobby Collins, this abrasive encounter was his first trip back to Goodison for a League fixture since his transfer two and a half years earlier. "It was diabolical . . . they blamed us, yet some Everton players were going over the ball time and time again. But the referee is in control of the game . . . it is up to him. When Sandy Brown got sent off, it was like a fuse on a bomb being lit . . . it really got a bit nasty and brutal. There were a lot of hard challenges that day. But you can't turn the other cheek or they'll kill you."

When the players did reappear ten minutes later on a pitch festooned with the cushions and rubbish thrown by the crowd, there was little let-up. Norman Hunter was booked in the second half and fouls – 32 in all – continued to be vicious. But Willie Bell's goal was sufficient to secure the match for Leeds, the fifth in a remarkable seven-match winning sequence. It came to an end with a 3-1 defeat at West Ham but thereafter Revie's men were unbeaten in their next 18 League games. The club that seemed destined for the Third Division three seasons before had become serious contenders for the League championship.

The habit of winning matches was also pushing the club towards its first FA Cup final. But, as ever, things were not straightforward; the manner in which victories were obtained brought Revie's men public castigation. A 3-0 win at Crystal Palace, who had been primed by manager Dick Graham to be as "hard" as their opponents, was only secured after a violent goal-less first half in which 17 fouls were committed. Three players, including Bremner, were booked. The first of two semi-final matches against Manchester United, played on a gluepot of a pitch, yielded no goals, 34 fouls, and bookings for Nobby Stiles and Denis Law. As some of these games developed their own harsh momentum, Revie, sitting on the sidelines, could not be held responsible for everything that took place on the pitch. Yet he was the father of Leeds' vigorous, physical style which, judged by results alone, had every justification. He had created the will to win and there was little evidence of him seeking to curb the excesses on the field of his talented but still somewhat immature envoys. Games such as those against Everton and Crystal Palace, or the bruising matches with Preston and Sunderland the previous season, would be remembered and held against his club. The press and others connected with the game were slow to give Revie's Leeds credit where it might have been due and frequently ignored the oft-heard pleas from Leeds' ranks that some players were more sinned against than sinners. With Revie, this rankled. He wanted to win but he also wanted to be liked.

Lord Harewood, Leeds United's president since 1961 and a keen amateur student of the game, had a strong sense of injustice about it all. "I think we always played to the strengths of the teams and not to the weaknesses. I'm not a great fan of the critics . . . I think at best they are a group of people who like to be in the majority, in the swim, and at worse, they're a pack of wolves or even hyenas. A lot of the criticism was untrue."

Harewood was sufficiently moved by his conviction that Leeds were being unfairly treated to study events in an away game at Chelsea. "I remember I was sitting next to Sir Alf Ramsey . . . he was not at all sympathetic towards Leeds. I was marking down the

71

fouls against us and the players by whom they were committed. After about 20 minutes, Billy Bremner's name was taken. But there had been six fouls on Bremner. Alf Ramsey looked down at my list and said: 'That's the kind of thing that gets a referee a bad name.' "

By any standards, the club's return to the First Division had been momentous. Leeds lost the League Championship to Manchester United by goal average with an end of season loss of form that would become distressingly familiar in future seasons. The club's final match against Birmingham City, who were bottom of the table, was notable for its bathos and eccentricity. Birmingham, down to ten men after just four minutes when winger Alex Jackson was injured, found Leeds in distracted, ineffectual mood, and had scored three goals without reply by the 50th minute. The pragmatic Revie, seeing his cause lost and the Cup final still to be contested, urged his players to save themselves. Instead, they fought back, Jack Charlton equalising two minutes before the end, and Norman Hunter hitting a post in injury time. The same evening, Manchester United beat Arsenal 2-1 to claim the title.

After the violence of the first encounter, the FA Cup semi-final replay against Manchester United was played in better spirit, and Leeds, showing remarkable defensive tenacity, withstood constant pressure before breaking out towards the end of the game then stealing victory as Billy Bremner headed in a free kick by Johnny Giles five minutes before time. Their reward was a Wembley encounter with Liverpool, something for which, despite all its combative enthusiasm, the team was ill-equipped. The side was infected with uncertainty and tension, qualities that also beset Revie; and while the players had grown up quickly, they were not seasoned, as were Liverpool, to cope with big set-piece occasions.

The Leeds supporters were inhibited too, outnumbered by boisterous, raucous Merseysiders. The story of the match, one of Wembley's dreariest finals, is well documented; the heroics of Liverpool left-back Gerry Byrne, who played almost all the match with a broken collar bone, Billy Bremner's improbable equaliser of Roger Hunt's extra time goal, before Ian St John gave Liverpool deserved victory in the 111th minute.

The players apologised to Revie for their anaemic performance.

© Colorsport

A personal triumph for Revie, elected Footballer of the Year in 1955 by the Football Writers' Association, despite Manchester City's last-gasp failures in the League and Cup.

On the way up . . . Revie (front row, fourth from left) in front of one of his mentors, Leicester City manager Johnny Duncan. While at Leicester, Revie married Duncan's niece, Elsie.

Revie's finest hour as a player – after being the last-minute choice for Manchester City's Cup-winning side against Birmingham City, 1956.

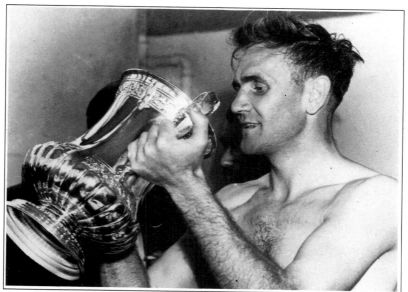

© Colorsport

Revie drinks deep from the cup that cheers. Honours at last for him and Manchester City, FA Cup winners, 1956.

© Yorkshire Post Newspaper Ltd

Don Revie signs for Leeds United watched by (left to right): Harold Marjason (Director), Cyril Williamson (Secretary) and Bill Lambton (Chief Trainer-Coach), November 1958.

Revie in action for Leeds United, 1958, shortly after signing for the club.

The team that Revie built . . . as youngsters. Coach Syd Owen (far left) and Revie (far right) flank their promising young recruits in 1961. These include Gary Sprake (back row, ninth from left); Paul Reaney (back row, 11th from left); Billy Bremner (second row, first left); Norman Hunter kneeling, bottom row, first left; and Terry Cooper, also kneeling, bottom row, extreme right.

© Colorsport

The most stunning defeat. Revie faces the camera after his Leeds team, odds-on favourites to beat Second Division Sunderland, are beaten 1-0 in one of Wembley's great upsets. Beside him is Billy Bremner and behind him the other players, dejected and bemused.

Don Revie shows off Leeds United's first hard-won trophy, the League Cup, in 1968. Leeds beat Arsenal 1-0 with a Terry Cooper goal in one of the dreariest matches seen at Wembley.

Get to them! Revie gees up his England players before the match against Czechoslovakia, the first in his reign as manager. England won 3-0.

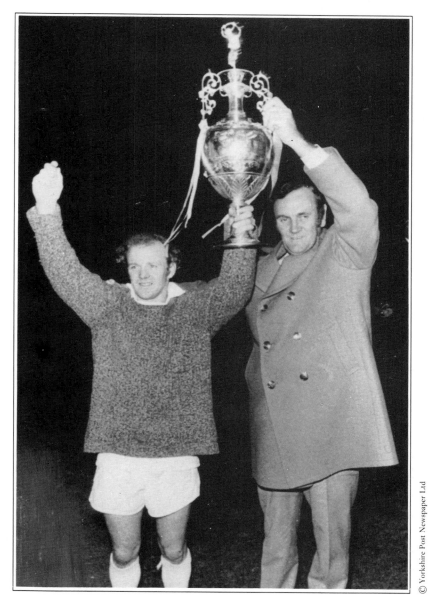

Don Revie and his captain, Billy Bremner, parade the League Championship trophy, May 1974, after Bremner's testimonial against Sunderland. This was Revie's final triumph with Leeds before leaving to manage England.

Revie, now crippled with Motor-Neurone disease, surrounded by his ex-players following a poignant reunion at Elland Road in 1988, the year before his death. He is flanked by Allan Clarke (left) and Billy Bremner (right), both kneeling, with Norman Hunter and David Harvey (front left), and Jack Charlton, Johnny Giles and Bobby Collins (far right) standing behind.

The gates of Elland Road draped with supporters' scarves as a tribute to Revie after his death in May 1989.

Revie in turn fed on his superstitions. Jim Storrie recalls hearing that one member of Revie's family had been to a fortune teller earlier in the season to be told Leeds would reach the Cup final but lose it. Margaret Veitch had attended the final, dressed in a turquoise outfit. She recalls: "On the way back, Don said, 'It's all your fault because you wore green.' " He may only have been half-joking, or not even joking at all. His most famous superstition was his continued wearing of a 'lucky' blue suit, notwithstanding its shabbiness in later years. But Revie's waking hours were riddled with other phobias and rituals; taking the same route to his dug out before a match, a fear of ornamental elephants, a readiness to believe that a gypsy curse on Elland Road was preventing his side winning, even a distaste for birds on pictures or as motifs.

Margaret Veitch's husband Peter remembers a visit Revie made to their home in Pudsey shortly after they had done some decorating. "We wanted to put some pictures up in the bedroom. The only ones I could get which were small were birds. He wouldn't go in the bedroom. He said: 'What are they doing there . . . you don't have birds in your house. You don't have birds anywhere.' That's the reason the peacock was eventually taken off the club badge. He wouldn't have birds."

Two years after the Liverpool final, Revie summoned a gypsy from Scarborough to Elland Road. Her mission was to exorcise whatever curse might be hanging over the ground and bringing his team ill-luck in crucial matches. Lord Harewood shared Revie's superstition about the possibility of peacocks bringing ill-luck. "You can't defy a known superstition," he says. "If you walk under a ladder, that's a dangerous thing to do . . . it's a metaphor for being hanged . . . in medieval times, people went under the ladder to be hanged. If you believe that to defy those things is a danger, then you are probably doing better not to defy them. I think Don's weakness was fear of not knowing everything there was to be known about the opposing side. That might have been carried to excess. The players may have been able to read more danger into situations than possibly existed."

In one season, Leeds United had come nearer to winning England's two principal domestic honours than ever before. Through craft and fight, the team had attained national recognition (albeit that much was unfavourable) and this was something quite new. In the 1950s the headlines had been garnered by John Charles; to the world beyond Leeds, it must sometimes have seemed as if the other ten players were merely an appendage to him. Revie's team was quite the reverse; a side without a star, without flamboyancy, and designed as such. Meanwhile the 1965-66 season gave it a new challenge, European competition in the form of the Inter Cities Fairs Cup; something ideal for the youthful hunger of Revie's players and also for gratifying Revie's dreams of creating a club of international status at Elland Road.

Revie's squad for the 1965-66 season remained basically unchanged, though in October he added to it Mike O'Grady, the Huddersfield Town right winger, for a fee of £45,000. The difference of approach at his new club made a forceful impact on O'Grady. "In training sessions at Huddersfield, if someone blew the whistle, it might take the players 10 minutes to get into line. At Leeds, it took 20 seconds. The training was sharp and varied; the five-a-sides competitive. Everything was so well organised," he says.

Once more, Leeds set about the First Division with serious purpose; and Europe in the same manner. Revie's players were a season older but still not without their rough edges. Billy Bremner in particular was in constant trouble with referees. He was to receive one of his many cautions during Leeds' 6-1 home victory over Northampton Town on 16 October, this time for dangerous play. Driven by the fear of losing Bremner to suspension once again, Revie approached the match referee Ray Tinkler and pleaded with him not to make an official record of the booking. He was given short shrift by Tinkler. By the time Bremner's case came up for an FA disciplinary commission in January, Revie found it judicious to write a letter confessing to the approach he had made. The FA viewed the matter with "deep concern" and insisted on an undertaking he should not try anything of the sort again. Revie, noted for calculated rather than impetuous behaviour said: "I acted in the heat of the moment, thinking about the possible consequences for Billy."

But there was a greater problem facing Revie that October when his skipper Bobby Collins broke a thigh during Leeds' first expedition abroad to play in the Fairs Cup. Collins was the victim of a reckless tackle during the first round second leg against Torino of Turin. Revie faced months without not only Collins' technical skills but also his inspiration. Yet Collins, at 34, was not finished. He still had enough fitness and appetite for the game to have ambitions of making a return; which he did less than eight months later in Leeds' final League match of the season at Manchester United. But it was clear to Revie that he had to make a major adjustment. His response was to switch Johnny Giles from outside right to Collins' midfield position from which, wearing the number ten shirt, Giles would operate in brilliant and irrepressible tandem with Bremner. If Giles's success was luck, then Revie had made his own luck by using intelligence and imagination. From this move, Giles achieved greatness though he was not an instant success; he had first to learn to play further forward than previously and also to deliver longer passes to front-runners instead of short square balls.

The FA Cup sapped little of Leeds United's energies that season. They were beaten by Chelsea in the fourth round. But up until Christmas Revie's team still looked a potent force in the championship race. Then a 1-0 defeat at Elland Road by Liverpool on 28 December left them forever in the wake of the Merseyside club. Leeds would be runners-up once more but six points behind Liverpool, a safe, unexciting distance. Their European adventure, however, continued to provide combustible matches. The third round Fairs Cup tie against Valencia at Elland Road on 2 February 1966 erupted into spectacular violence 15 minutes from time with the tie at 1-1. Jack Charlton, now captaining Leeds, had advanced in support of a Leeds attack when he was kicked by a Spanish defender. Then he was punched; and then, in his own words, he lost his head. The brawl that ensued brought police on to the pitch, and, for the second time in little over a year, Leeds and their opponents were taken off the field by the referee so that rage and fury might subside. The match ended with Charlton and two Spaniards being sent off.

The controversy rumbled on long after the final whistle. In its midst were Revie and Dutch referee Leo Horn who, in Peter Lorimer's view, had lost control of the game. According to Horn, Revie had begged him not to send Charlton off with the words: "Do you know what you are doing? He is an international." Revie, fresh from the FA disciplinary hearing involving his approach to referee Ray Tinkler over the Billy Bremner caution, denied the exchange ever took place. In any event, Mr Horn did not referee the return leg in Spain, for which forecasts of horrific combat had been made. Instead, there was a disciplined performance by Leeds whose 1-0 victory emphasised a growing maturity. Yet the Spanish still seemed to have a gift for provoking Revie's players. The Fairs Cup semi-final saw them drawn against Real Zaragoza, a team both mean and talented; and four minutes from the end of the first leg in Spain, Johnny Giles, who had sustained the brutal attentions of numerous Spanish players, was sent off for barging a defender. Ultimately, Leeds were to be outclassed by Zaragoza, losing the semi-final play-off 3-1 at Elland Road after the first two matches ended even on aggregate.

A pattern of contesting at least one major trophy each season had been established by Revie's team and would last until the end of his reign at Elland Road, along with the framework of the team that would sustain him through those years. The comings and goings, the short-term *ad hoc* buys were largely a thing of the past. If anything, in 1966 and 1967, there was a feeling among some supporters that Revie was standing still, an impatience that players of flair had not been bought to spice up the team and leaven some dull performances. Yet Revie had taken part in clandestine negotiations to try and lure Alan Ball from Blackpool to Elland Road; his dream was to create a dynamic midfield of Ball, Giles and Bremner with which few First Division clubs could have lived.

Revie had been monitoring Ball's progress since he was a teenager playing for Blackpool reserves. The Leeds manager's allegedly irregular approaches to Ball, who was in dispute with Blackpool over the terms of a new contract, were described in the player's autobiography eleven years later. In his book, Ball claimed he had secret meetings with Revie in which the Leeds manager encouraged him to continue his dispute with Blackpool. Any money he might lose by not signing, Revie would make up to him. According to Ball, the Leeds manager was as good as his word and paid him £300, in three instalments, during their secret meetings on the Yorkshire moors. Meanwhile Ball, who had enhanced his value by a memorably vigorous performance in the World Cup final was also being chased by Everton. As the

Merseyside club came in with a bid of £110,000 Revie was still struggling to persuade his directors to go above £100,000. "Give me time, Alan," Ball claims Revie said. But in the end, Ball grew tired of waiting. Everton were a big club with potential and he was happy to agree terms with them. Revie was to tell one journalist that he was moved to tears by the extent of his disappointment.

The story as told by Ball showed neither him nor Revie in good light. The Football Association responded by charging both with bringing the game into disrepute: Ball on the grounds that he had received approaches and payments as an inducement to leave one club and join another in contravention of Football League and FA rules. In 1979, he was subsequently fined £3,000 by an FA tribunal, but the case against Revie, who denied Ball's stories and the charge, was left pending, awaiting the result of the libel case Revie was at that time conducting against the *Daily Mirror* and its saga of his alleged attempts to fix crucial matches. But ultimately Revie never went to court to clear his name. Ball, invited to discuss these and other encounters with Revie, has declined to elaborate.

Revie's men galloped off in search of more glory as the 1966-67 season started. Familiar patterns asserted themselves once more; the occasional tempestuous match, over-caution away from home, and bad luck with injuries and referees. The away game at Burnley was not out of the ordinary for Revie's men. They went into the match with five key players injured: Jack Charlton, Bobby Collins, Mike O'Grady, Alan Peacock and Jimmy Greenhoff. Revie's youth squad showed its undoubted value: in came 18-year-old Mick Bates for his League début at inside-right; Eddie Gray, also 18, at inside-left; Peter Lorimer, 19, at outside right; Paul Madeley, 21, at centre-forward against a potent and full-strength Burnley who had finished third the previous season. Eddie Gray scored in a fierce 1-1 draw during which five players were booked and the on-field aggression spread to the Turf Moor crowd. In the second half, referee Stokes threatened to abandon the match unless spectators stopped hurling missiles on to the pitch. Such was life, sometimes, when Revie's raw young men were pitched into battle against a seasoned enemy.

Injuries to key players undoubtedly disrupted Leeds. Mike O'Grady played in just a third of the 42 League matches; Alan Peacock would play only six League games all season; Bobby

Collins made just seven appearances before being given a free transfer to Bury. Leeds were never to be serious contenders for the League Championship, and finished fourth – again with 55 points – behind Manchester United, Liverpool and Tottenham. They also made a stunning departure from the League Cup, beaten 7-0 by West Ham United at Upton Park. Revie lavished his congratulations on West Ham (his habit of immediately showering praise on the victorious opposition was seen by some observers as slick public relations, by others as illustrating an intense desire to be liked), then turned on his own shattered team. Never again would they lose in such a fashion, he ordered. Neither did they.

Leeds were to make much sterner challenges in the FA Cup and, once again, in the Inter Cities Fairs Cup. Urged on by Revie, some of his walking wounded took to the field against their will. Billy Bremner, whose courage and tenacity has never been in question, recalls: "Over the years, a good 70 per cent of the lads have played in games where they shouldn't have done. I remember the Cup game against Sunderland that season. I had had my knee ligaments done at Southampton the previous Saturday. A week for knee ligaments is impossible . . . there is no way you can do it. When the team went up on Friday and I was on the team sheet, I thought: 'I don't believe this'."

"We went up to Sunderland the night before. At ten o'clock in the morning, Les Cocker came to my room and said: 'Billy, we're going to have a fitness test.' We went down and Les did a couple of block tackles on me and nearly killed me. I came off and said: 'There's no way I can play, honestly.' But the boss said: 'I'd rather have you with one leg than anybody else with two.' So I went out and played, and I tell you, I had a disaster. I stayed out on the right wing most of the game. After, the boss said: 'I didn't have you out there to play you know.' I said: 'For Christ's sake, what did you have me out there for?' He said it was to gee the other lads up, that they would have dipped without me. I thought: 'What a load of bullshit!' "

Peter Lorimer recalls Revie's use of injured players in later years. "It didn't always work out for him. When we played at Wolves after the 1972 Cup final, Johnny Giles was only 80 per cent fit. I don't think it was to our benefit. When you're fresh you can carry an injury; when you're tired, you can't. I've seen the boss myself tell the doctor a player will be alright when I'm sure the doctor didn't think he would be fit."

Revie also had an oblique manner in team selection that sometimes disconcerted his loyal players. Bobby Collins, having fought his way back to fitness after breaking his leg against Torino, recalls being dropped quite out of the blue by Revie. "I didn't particularly like that. At least when it happened at Everton, Harry Catterick gave me some warning." On another occasion, again without warning, Revie informed Collins that Blackpool wanted to sign him and then promptly dropped him for the next game. "I couldn't understand it. I didn't want to go to bloody Blackpool," Collins says. In the event, the move came to nothing and it was at his own request that Collins was granted a free transfer to Bury. His last game for Leeds was in the 3-0 home victory over Stoke City on 11 February. "I played a blinder!" Collins says.

When Revie felt that Peter Lorimer was playing below his usual standard, his method was to tell him he thought he looked tired and needed a rest. It worked. "He was very clever and calculating . . . he would read situations," Lorimer says. "I thought I wasn't playing badly but he felt I needed a kick up the backside. The week after, I'd find myself back in the team. With other people, he would have to be harder."

By 1966-67, Lorimer could class himself a regular. He made 27 League appearances and two as substitute following his 34 in the previous campaign. He was to be the focal point of the most memorable incident involving Leeds United that season, in the FA Cup semi-final against Chelsea. The cup run that year was fulfilling one of Revie's ambitions for the club by attracting large crowds to Elland Road: 41,329 for the fourth round 5-0 victory over West Bromwich Albion; then a ground record attendance of 57,892 for the fifth round replay against Sunderland. That night, 15 March 1967, Elland Road was dangerously, crushingly full, for there had been insufficient time to make the match all-ticket. After two 1-1 draws it took a second replay at Boothferry Park, Hull, for Leeds to overcome Sunderland. They won 2-1 and with order restored at the Elland Road turnstiles for the sixth round, 48,887 watched the home side beat Manchester City with a second half goal from Jack Charlton. The semi-final against Chelsea at Villa Park, watched by more than 62,000, is famed less for the first half header by Tony Hateley that settled it in Chelsea's favour than for the thunderous Lorimer equaliser-that-never-was – a last minute shot of theatrical velocity from a short, square free kick by Johnny Giles which was disallowed by referee Ken Burns because Chelsea players were not ten yards from the ball.

The anguish and indignation of Revie and his players was easy to understand, and Ken Burns' action was to establish a pattern of grotesque refereeing decisions that would thwart Leeds in key games over the following years.

But at least Leeds' progress in Europe was less rumbustious than in the previous season, despite another meeting with Valencia in the third round of the Fairs Cup. Leeds' second leg 2-0 victory in Spain on 8 February (they won the tie 3-1 on aggregate) was achieved with several key players injured. Into the side Revie drafted Rod Belfitt at centre-forward and Terry Hibbitt, another talented product of the Elland Road youth policy. Goals from Giles and Lorimer won the match and the tie for Leeds who had played with notable skill and discipline in defence.

In the fourth round Leeds had a slice of luck. Outplayed for much of their two legs by the Italian club Bologna, the tie, drawn 1-1 on aggregate, was settled in Revie's favour by the toss of a coin. Leeds had substantially less trouble beating Kilmarnock 4-2 on aggregate in the semi-final but the final, held over to the beginning of the following season, paired them with the Yugoslavian side Dynamo Zagreb, among Europe's most accomplished teams. Revie was in awe of them; too much so, Mike O'Grady feels. Leeds had lost the first leg in Yugoslavia 2-0 and players anticipated a bold approach to try and save the tie. "But instead, he was really cautious, despite the away result," O'Grady says. "For one thing, he had Paul Reaney on the right wing but also he filled our heads with the opposition. I was a winger yet he was warning me about the other winger . . . expecting me to operate defensively as well as up front. You'd be sitting there thinking: 'God, just let us play!' " As it happened, the Yugoslavs hardly allowed Leeds the opportunity, freezing them out with possession football to gain a 0-0 draw and the trophy.

It was not a good start to the 1967-68 season by Revie's team; quite the sort to nourish his superstitious forebodings. Yet morale among his players remained surprisingly high. For Peter Lorimer defeat was simply something you got over. Johnny Giles believes that one reason Revie's Leeds side stayed together so long was because of the momentous disappointments it sustained. "People didn't give us enough credit for picking it up," he says. "After what we had been through, a lot of clubs, a lot of players would have collapsed. But there were never any public recriminations. Everyone kept quiet and we said we'd start again next year. We knew we were the best team in the country." Syd Owen recalls: "We would just tell the players that they had done themselves justice."

Billy Bremner, whom Revie had made captain in an effort to help quell the worst excesses of the young Scot's temperament on the field, recalls his manager's adroit manner in keeping valued players at the club. "When you'd come to the end of the season, you'd get options on your contract. I would go in and ask for a rise. Then just as I'd walk in, he'd say, 'Wee man, I just want a word with you. I'm going to increase your money', and then tell you the amount. I thought: 'I wasn't going to ask for that much . . . that's brilliant.' You'd walk out of his office thinking 'I've done it' but then a bit later, you'd suddenly think: 'He's done you. He's got you under contract again, but you think he's a good guy because he's upped your wages!' "

After an indifferent first few games, during which grumbles persisted among supporters about Revie's failure to buy a proven goalscorer, Leeds started running into form, though the club programme notes written in advance of Leeds' home match with Leicester City on 23 September reflected the fans' concern. Just after Revie had declared there would be no panic buying, he responded with a bold and astute purchase. At £100,000 from Sheffield United, centre-forward Mick Jones was, by far, Leeds United's most expensive acquisition but he would repay the Leeds manager with years of brave, unselfish performances. Two weeks later, Revie's team served dramatic notice on the rest of the football world that not only could it defend and trade kick for kick, but that also it was capable of brilliance. The victims were Chelsea, confused and vulnerable after the controversial departure of their manager Tommy Docherty the previous night. As if smelling easy meat, Leeds tore into the London side. In their 7-0 victory, Bremner, making his last appearance before a 28-day suspension, shone above all others, crowning a virtuoso display with the final goal, an enthralling overhead kick.

At the beginning of the season Revie had made another significant amendment to his team, drafting in Terry Cooper at left-back in place of Willie Bell. Cooper had been at the club five years and grown increasingly frustrated at his inability to command a regular first-team place. Revie had seemed ambivalent about Cooper, whom he had converted from left-wing to full-back, and indeed had nearly sold him to Blackburn Rovers. That Rovers could not bring themselves to spend £25,000 was Revie's good fortune. In the following years, he was aghast to think how cheaply he might have parted with Cooper's talents. The former left-winger's attacking instincts were to remain with him and he added a potent, attractive new dimension to Revie's team.

That season, which in September saw Harry Reynolds resign as Leeds chairman on grounds of ill health, had Leeds fighting for honours on four fronts. It emphasised the grand scale of Revie's ambition but certain key matches would expose again a curious timidity of approach. In 1968, Leeds United at last won a trophy of significance, the League Cup, in a manner that stressed the winning of it, rather than the style of victory, mattered most to a team that had lost out on so much. The players may have been more durable than Revie appreciated but he doubted their capacity to sustain further disappointments. A goal from Terry Cooper after 20 minutes won Leeds the trophy, his splendid volley representing the only score and most of the colour in a drab, irritable match against Arsenal. Once in the lead, Revie's men were prepared to defend and contain, as they were in other matches that season, to the aggrievement of opposing teams and spectators alike. With Cooper and Eddie Gray now playing regularly, Revie's team had two more stylists but only sporadically would they have the opportunity to give their talents full expression.

But winning was a habit until, ultimately, the pressures of 65 matches took their toll. Again, Revie's team progressed to the FA Cup semi-final, and again lost by a single goal. This time they could not blame a rogue referee; instead, they engineered their own defeat as Jack Charlton conceded a penalty, handling a goal-bound shot from Jimmy Husband presented to him by a poor clearance from Gary Sprake. While their away form in

League matches had not been good, Leeds remained serious contenders for the Championship until losing the final four matches of the season. They were to end up fourth, with 53 points, five fewer than champions Manchester City.

There was, however, rich consolation in European competition. There had been great value to Revie's men in playing a succession of bruising, impassioned matches over the previous three years, although their passage to the 1967-68 Fairs Cup final was less arduous than in earlier tournaments; the opposition in the latter rounds were all from Scotland: Hibernian, Glasgow Rangers and Dundee. Again fixture congestion meant the two-legged final had to be played early the following season. Leeds' opponents, the Hungarian side Ferencvaros, had awesome ability but the first leg at Elland Road showed they could also cut up rough when a goal down. A lone Mick Jones header sustained Revie's team, now utterly masterful at stone-wall defending, despite frenzied pressure by Ferencvaros in the away leg. It ended goal-less and Revie, for whom the final minutes seemed like hours, claimed his second trophy in six months.

The trophy was won on 11 September 1968, a splendid early fillip for Revie's team. Yet before the season started, Revie, in typical cajoling gee-'em-up fashion, had told his players they were going to win the League Championship and do so without losing a League match.

The team went unbeaten for the first nine League matches before losing 3-1 at Manchester City on 28 September. They swiftly recovered their equilibrium, winning the next three matches before being quite humiliated in a 5-1 defeat at Burnley, a result few would have predicted; and fewer still might have guessed it would be Leeds' last defeat of the season, as their recovery started with modest uncertainty in successive goal-less draws against West Bromwich Albion, Manchester United and Tottenham.

For once, Revie's men had their heads less full of other competitions. By 16 October they were out of the League Cup, having been beaten 2-1 at Crystal Palace in the fourth round, and by January Sheffield Wednesday ensured an early departure from the FA Cup by beating Leeds 3-1 at Elland Road in a third-round replay. They were not, however, to shrug off the Fairs Cup so easily. The second round paired Leeds with the Italian club

Napoli and entailed a singularly vicious November encounter in Naples. Leeds lost the match 2-0, drew the tie 2-2 and won through on the toss of a coin, but post-match rancour was, once again, the main story. Revie, although hardened against the slings and arrows of outrageous continental foul play, exclaimed in a club programme: "I hope I never have to take a team there again!" It had been another of those matches in which Leeds players were ritually kicked off the ball. Revie and the Leeds board met to consider whether the club should continue playing in European football. Club chairman Alderman Percy Woodward said while the money was welcome, the safety of the players was far more important . . . the club was lucky no-one had received an injury that could have put him out of the game for several weeks.

By 19 March, as the League title challenge intensified, Leeds had been banished from Europe by Ujpest Dozsa, beaten comprehensively in both legs by a 3-0 aggregate. But their domestic campaign had gained a formidable head of steam; seven successive victories from 24 January to 8 March in which just three goals were conceded. "Avoid defeat today, and the title's yours," Revie would say to his team before every match during the run-in. And for once, Revie's team's luck was not all bad. A 1-0 victory against Queens Park Rangers at Loftus Road in January owed much to good fortune in a match during which Leeds had been run ragged by a home side desperately seeking points to avoid relegation. Rangers suffered all the misfortunes of the struggling underdog; they missed a penalty, they twice hit the woodwork, and Leeds stole two points. In an earlier home game against Manchester United, Johnny Giles deflected an indirect free kick from George Best into his own net. This time Leeds' opponents had cause to be upset by the vagaries of match officials; what seemed a good goal was disallowed by Swansea referee Bill Gow.

The League Championship was finally won on the night of 28 April after a goal-less draw with Liverpool at Anfield, yet a 2-1 victory at Arsenal 16 days earlier probably put the matter beyond reasonable doubt. The match was almost a microcosm of Leeds' season; sporadically violent, an illustration of the team's proficiency in defence and tactical ingenuity, a game in which luck helped secure two invaluable points. The team's first good fortune was that Gary Sprake was allowed to stay longer than four minutes on the pitch after punching Arsenal centre-forward Bobby Gould on the jaw – Sprake's summary way of repaying Gould's foul challenge for a high ball. Perhaps the greater slice of luck for Leeds was the erratic form of Arsenal centre-half Ian Ure who presented the visitors with both goals through defensive blunders. He first misjudged a high clearance by Mick Bates, allowing Mick Jones to run through and score. Then, after Arsenal equalised, Ure hit a back-pass wide of goalkeeper Bob Wilson, allowing Johnny Giles to gain possession near the by-line and walk the ball into the net. What Leeds had won they were determined to hold, even if it was not pretty to watch. In the dying minutes, they passed the ball around among themselves or dallied with it down by the corner flag, intent at all costs on depriving Arsenal of possession. One Sunday newspaper journalist wrote afterwards: "It is a pity that Leeds, so near to a championship they unquestionably deserve, chose to parade their infuriating time-wasting tactics near the end." But that was the way Revie's men knew. While the Leeds manager was interested in good public relations off the field, perhaps by way of atonement for some of his players' meaner performances, he had endured too many disappointments to wish to change Leeds' unappealing safety-first tactics and jeopardise, so late on, the chance of winning football's greatest domestic prize.

The game at Anfield, where Leeds achieved the point they needed in what was another rather sterile encounter, is remembered more for the post-match generosity of the Liverpool supporters on the Kop in applauding the new champions; for, hard though it may be to imagine 21 years later, Leeds supporters had made little impression on the occasion. Attendances at Elland Road that season had been healthy, around 37,000, but often, to Revie's intense frustration, lacking in passion. He yearned for bigger crowds, 50,000 at a time, more noise, some adulation for the club he had created. His achievements, in so short a time, were immense; the success of 1968-69 was based on great consistency. Sprake, Reaney, Bremner and Hunter played in every game, Jack Charlton missed just one, Mick Jones only two, Mike O'Grady, who had had the most glorious season of his injury-hit career, played in all but four matches. They were a team most opponents dreaded playing. But they had yet to be loved.

Chapter Seven

AT LAST Revie, voted Manager of the Year following Leeds United's extraordinary efforts, could be reassured that the side he had created was not afflicted by some flaw that would always deny it the highest honours. Three trophies in 13 months had, if anything, further fuelled his irrepressible ambition. They had also made him a target for an old continental adversary, Torino. In May 1969 the Italian club offered Leeds United £70,000 to buy out Revie's contract, which had six and a half years to run. To Revie himself they were offering around £24,000, a further monthly salary, bonuses, and a crash course in Italian. But Torino were told by Leeds chairman Alderman Percy Woodward that the manager's contract was beyond price. Revie, perhaps mindful of the fact that if he had created the club, the club had also created him, told journalists he would stay at Elland Road "for the rest of my life as a manager. I want us all to stick together at Leeds . . . our targets are the European Cup and the World Club championship. I don't think we've reached our peak yet and if we keep working at it, the best years for Leeds can still be those to come."

In Italian football, the most successful sides were those who tended to give least away and officials from Torino would have been impressed by the rearguard that Revie had constructed at Leeds. His side had won the League Championship with just two defeats, 26 goals conceded, but on the other hand only 66 were scored. With another of his occasional flourishes, Revie acted. His aim was to bring more colour and scoring potential to Elland Road, and so, in the close season, he broke the British transfer record by recruiting to Leeds the Leicester striker Allan Clarke at a cost of £165,000.

It would be the club's most tumultuous season. The defeats and near-misses of previous years would be almost as nothing compared to Leeds United's sufferings in March and April 1970, as a season which had held the richest promise disintegrated amid fixture congestion and player fatigue, with the intoxicating prospect of scooping the major trophies coming to nothing. It was a season also that showed the football world that Leeds were not merely efficient, they were capable of playing with awesome, brilliant authority. The championship season had exorcised absolute caution from the players' make-up.

Soon after Allan Clarke arrived, Mike O'Grady, who had served with distinction on the right-wing during the previous campaign, departed. He had not intended leaving Elland Road and remains a little bemused by elements of Revie's behaviour leading up to his transfer to Wolverhampton Wanderers. "I'd had my best year, clear of injury though I started off the pre-season in 1969 with a carbuncle underneath my foot," O'Grady says. "I thought I wouldn't get back in the team . . . but to my surprise I did, though I didn't play very well. We had a chat and Don said he didn't think I was fit enough. So I played in the reserves. I thought, "He wants me to go." Then he told me Wolves wanted to buy me. I said I didn't want to go. But he came up again and said that Bill McGarry, the Wolves manager wanted to see me. So I travelled down to Wolves and signed. It was the biggest mistake of my life. I wasn't happy and I didn't like the set up."

O'Grady considers Revie might have wanted to get rid of him because he was the only first-team regular who was single. Always intensely interested in the welfare of his players, Revie had already asked O'Grady why he didn't get married. Revie, O'Grady feels, thought single players were potentially troublesome, that they were more liable to go out and get involved in some sort of a scrape. Moreover, Revie liked conformity and leaned towards family establishments. His own family life had been dislocated first by the death of his mother in his boyhood, then by his departure to Leicester when only 16. Margaret Veitch says that because of his early upbringing, Revie didn't feel as if he had a proper family life at all. "That's why he made such a lot of fuss of Elsie's aunts, uncles, brother and sister."

Peter Veitch says: "The family that he wanted was the football team. They were his children . . . and their children his grandchildren . . . that's the kind of attitude he took." Revie developed friendships with people who had a stable family life. "He didn't want to know about the people who were in the throes of divorce or who had anything rocky in their marriage," Margaret Veitch says. "In earlier years, I regarded him as a brother and he regarded me as a sister. When my marriage split up, he was very sad. Then Peter came on the scene and Don said: 'I've got to meet this bloke and see whether he is alright.' "

The complexity that some perceived in Revie's character came because he could not cope with instability, Peter Veitch feels. People to whom Revie displayed coolness were likely to be those who did not give him a sense of being comfortable. But the Veitches share with Bobby Collins the belief that Revie, though he behaved in ways that suggested a complex make-up, was essentially simple. "Elsie was a sophisticate in that she was better educated than he was," says Peter Veitch. "But that's no disrespect . . . he admired education."

However much the Revies believed in the warmth and intimacy of family life, they eventually took the decision to send both Duncan and Kim away to school. Part of the decision in Duncan's case was the stress of living with Leeds United, which made a distressing impact on Revie when, after Leeds' FA Cup semi-final defeat against Chelsea in 1967, he encountered his tearful son outside Villa Park. The notion of uprooting him from Leeds Grammar School to Repton, 80 miles from home, distressed both father and son. When they arrived, with Duncan in tears, Revie was all for taking him home. It was Elsie who intervened firmly, who said "No". Margaret Veitch recalls: "Don did say to me once, 'Kim's not going away.' But she did, a couple of years later."

Peter Veitch considers Elsie felt the children being at home was a domestic complication. "I think she wished to concentrate more on Don . . . any advancement Don made in life brought her along with it. She wished him to get his true value. At the end of the day, she enjoyed being a celebrity. If she had been faced with having to bring the children up, she wouldn't have been able to concentrate on Don . . . she realised he had potential and she was trying to help him along. Don was basically a naïve sort of a man. In getting the children away to put Don down the right path in life, they would all benefit."

Meanwhile Revie was letting his players perform with fewer inhibitions on the pitch. The team was already held in awe elsewhere, despite having been wont to pay exaggerated respect to mediocre opposition, as Mike O'Grady discovered soon after joining Wolves. "They said they were frightened of Leeds. They thought we were hard, that they would always get put under pressure." O'Grady found that his former club was a source of constant fascination among his new team-mates. "They were always asking me about Leeds. Then when I had been there a few weeks, Bill McGarry got sick of it. He told me to stop talking about them." How Revie's heart might have been gladdened, had he known.

His side did not make its most distinguished start to a new season in 1969-70. Having at last won the championship, Revie could detect the side lacked its usual hunger. Everton, however, opened with a tremendous surge of winning form. The two sides met at Goodison Park on 30 August and, faced by the home side's fluid potent football, Leeds found themselves three goals down by half time. It was a sharp shock that suddenly seemed to bring them to their senses. They made a fight of the second half, pulling goals back though Bremner and Clarke, though not quite able to retrieve the match. Thereafter, Revie's side went through its next 18 League matches unbeaten.

The new swaggering style of Revie's men was seen by most people for the first time in their opening European Cup tie. The opponents, part-timers Lyn Oslo, were easy meat but few expected them to be destroyed so completely. When, on 17 September, the Norwegian side ventured to Elland Road, they found themselves five goals down by half time, ten at full time. Never in the history of the competition had one side used another so cruelly for the purpose of sharpening its wits. The return leg in Oslo provided respite of a sort: Leeds managed only six goals. The 16-nil aggregate was a record for the European Cup. In November, Leeds were drawn against Ferencvaros, about whom they knew much more. But the Hungarian side came in for the same treatment, albeit on a more modest scale. Beaten 3-0 at Elland Road, they showed little stomach for the return leg in which Revie's men helped themselves to another three goals without reply.

The new year began for Revie with the award of the OBE for his services to football. Certainly the form his team was striking might have led him to believe it was some sort of a lucky talisman. On 10 January a television audience of millions saw one of the most prodigious performances that Leeds United had ever given. The opponents were Chelsea and Leeds' show was played out before a largely hostile audience of 57,221, at Stamford Bridge. The Londoners were a good side, in form and in third place; and sufficiently inspired by the occasion to take a 2-1 lead by half time. No-one could have envisaged what was in store for them in the 45 minutes that followed. Leeds martialled their forces and dictated the game in a manner that had many, including television commentators, groping for words, as they played with a power, assurance and authority that the English game had rarely seen. The 2-1 deficit had turned into a 5-2 victory by full time. Chelsea had not disintegrated; they had simply run into a force which, that afternoon, neither they nor probably any other team could have survived.

Leeds had extracted revenge against Everton a fortnight earlier, winning 2-1 at Elland Road. There was nothing to suggest that their appetite for a second successive League championship was still jaded. In the New Year they turned their attentions to the FA Cup, the one domestic trophy that had so far eluded Revie. His team made heavy work of beating Swansea 2-1 at Leeds in the third round. Their next opponents were Sutton United, amateurs in the Isthmian League, a pairing that delighted those who relished fantastic possibilities. But while Revie was now allowing his team to display their technical accomplishments on the pitch, he could not abandon his obsession with planning. Sutton United, like every other side, were closely watched, both by Syd Owen and a London-based scout, and dossiers were prepared with Owen's usual thoroughness. Moreover, Revie was intent on knowing every detail about the lay-out of Sutton's modest stadium and was jolted by news reaching him shortly before the match that the club had ordered hundreds of extra seats to be placed around the pitch. Revie's disquiet, based partly on fear for the safety of his players, surprised the Sutton officials who, anxious to maintain good relations, invited representatives from Leeds to inspect the ground on the eve of the match.

If Sutton nourished any dreams of glory beyond staging the fixture and drawing 14,000 to their ground at Gander Green Lane, they were not to last long. They became the latest in a succession of opponents to be crushed by the concentrated, acute football of Revie's men. Within an hour Leeds had done their work, scoring six goals and conceding none. For one Sutton player though, centre-half John Faulkner, the day was indeed momentous. Revie had been so impressed by his efforts at policing Mick Jones and Allan Clarke that two months later he signed him as cover for Jack Charlton.

Leeds' League form continued to hold up through January and February: since the defeat at Everton they had lost only once, 2-1 at Newcastle, on Boxing Day. They were making inexorable, if sometimes unspectacular, progress in the FA Cup. The fifth round home tie with Mansfield was won 2-0 in laboured fashion. At Swindon in the sixth round, the keen edge and old composure returned. The Leeds defence absorbed Swindon's best efforts for the first half hour before Allan Clarke struck twice in three minutes. His two piercing attacks ended the match as a contest.

By March, Leeds' season was coming rapidly to the boil. The League programme had started earlier than normal, on 9 August, so that the England party for the World Cup could acclimatise and prepare adequately for its trip to Mexico. The final League fixtures of the domestic programme were scheduled for 21 April. While Everton, Leeds' principal challengers for the League title, were undistracted by other competitions in the closing stages of the season, it was clear that Revie's men were about to encounter a fixture pile-up. The problems were magnified on 14 March when Leeds and Manchester United were unable to settle their FA Cup semi-final. A goal-less draw, in which Manchester United had often looked the better side, was followed by another no scoring encounter, entailing extra time, nine days later at Villa Park. They had just three days respite before a third debilitating clash at Bolton, a game in which Leeds players transcended their fatigue and Billy Bremner scored the only goal.

Earlier in the month Leeds had already played two stern and demanding games in their European Cup quarter final against the Belgian club Standard Liege. There had been some evidence of the team's tiredness in the second leg at Elland Road where Leeds repeated the hard-earned 1-0 victory they had gained in Belgium the previous week. By the time of the Easter Saturday League fixture against Southampton, even Revie felt half his team were unfit for battle. While there had been no weakening in Leeds' League form, his priorities remained the FA Cup, which he came so close to winning five years earlier, and the European Cup, the grandest prize of all.

Although Revie's half-strength side gained an early lead, it was soon overhauled by Southampton who eventually beat their listless opponents 3-1. The championship was still possible but at this point Revie elected to concede to Everton. However, the decision was not shared with the 41,011 spectators who turned up for the Easter Monday away game against Derby County to discover the Leeds manager was fielding a travesty of a side; an entire team of reserves. The remaining energy of his star players was to be conserved for Cup battle. The Derby match was lost 4-1; probably all Revie deserved.

In so doing, Revie incurred, not for the first time, the displeasure of Football League secretary Alan Hardaker. Over the previous two years, Hardaker had tired of Revie's requests for fixture rearrangements and postponements that might put Leeds at an advantage. In football matters Revie was, in Hardaker's opinion, devious, selfish and ruthless, and would cut corners to get his own way. Revie had offended Hardaker the previous season by an oblique approach to the League secretary's subordinates, with the aim of bringing forward by 24 hours a League Cup tie against Bristol City. It was the impropriety of Revie seeking to involve his juniors that had made Hardaker especially indignant. On another occasion, Hardaker gave Revie short shrift when the Leeds manager asked for a postponement because three of his key players were badly injured. Hardaker noted drily that not only did all three make sufficiently miraculous recoveries to play, but one scored twice and another was, by general consent, the man of the match.

According to Hardaker, part of Revie's fixture pile-up was of his own making; earlier in the season, he had had fixtures put off. Revie's escapade in flouting League regulations by fielding a weakened team against Derby County cost the club a £5,000 fine but the Leeds manager was unrepentant. Hardaker meanwhile was excoriated by many in Leeds for the club's failure to win a trophy in 1970.

Their mutual antipathy also extended to the appointment of referees. Hardaker had taken particular exception to another of Revie's oblique approaches, through a club administrator, wondering whether a referee for Leeds' next match might be changed. Again, Hardaker's reply was terse; that clubs were not, whatever the event, free to select their own officials. Revie's determination to do everything in his power that might bring Leeds an advantage was noted, yet not deplored, by the leading referee of the time, Jack Taylor. "He always looked at every angle. I don't blame him, he had a job to do. His knowledge was so good. He knew the referees. He was the ultimate tactician."

Revie, Taylor felt, would try to arrange for personal hearings for players facing suspension to be held at a time that would benefit the club, or at any rate, harm it the least. Taylor has memories of Revie turning up to one such hearing saying he had filmed "evidence" that what Taylor had done was wrong. When, hinting the material could have been doctored, Taylor asked Revie if he was producing the entire film of the incident, the Leeds manager appeared quite hurt. "He said he would never do anything like that," Taylor recalls.

Taylor, a figure of the footballing establishment, nevertheless had a reputation for firmness and sound judgement. While Hardaker claimed Revie grew uneasy at the prospect of being refereed by the strongest officials, the Leeds manager had in fact requested that Taylor, who had controlled the first two FA Cup semi-final clashes against Manchester United, should also be in charge for the second replay. These were epic matches involving some volatile players and much was at stake but Taylor never allowed them to get out of hand.

The fiasco of the match against Derby County had allowed Revie's first team two days to patch themselves up for their

European Cup semi-final against Glasgow Celtic. On 1 April they took the field at Elland Road and were behind within a minute. The strains of the season were painfully obvious; the defending tired and uncertain, the assured potency lacking. For once, Norman Hunter, whose heart and stamina so often buttressed Leeds, was missing injured. The confidence, and nearly all the danger, came from Celtic. Leeds played the rest of the game as if stunned by the early goal they had conceded. A trip to Glasgow two weeks later beckoned along with a 1-0 deficit that looked insurmountable.

And yet when it came to the FA Cup final against Chelsea on 11 April, the club seemed to summon from nowhere its old vim. Revie's side achieved everything but victory. On a heavily sanded pitch that caused some strange bounces of the ball, Leeds produced their stylish, muscular football once again. Told by Revie to go out and play, they responded with one of the best post-war exhibitions of football Wembley had seen. Eddie Gray unfurled a performance of tormenting skill on the left wing, reducing Chelsea right-back David Webb to impotence. Other Chelsea defenders floundered in spaces where Leeds men had been. Yet the capricious bounce of the ball that had helped Jack Charlton's early header squirt over the goal-line and give Leeds the lead would work against them, and was possibly to blame for Gary Sprake allowing a low, not markedly venomous, shot to squirm under his body and put Chelsea level. Sheer lack of concentration squandered the seemingly unassailable advantage that Mick Jones's goal seven minutes from time had given Leeds, as a free kick taken quickly three minutes later allowed Ian Hutchinson to sneak into a vacant defence and produce the first draw after extra time in a final for 58 years.

More cruel, stamina-sapping punishment for Revie's team! A 2-2 draw, a replay, and Celtic to be faced at Hampden Park before a 136,000 crowd in which Yorkshire voices were hardly to be heard, blown away by the Celtic cacophony. Yet if the support was timid, the team still had guts and fight. With Bremner's early goal that levelled the tie, Revie and his team were momentarily teased by the mirage of victory. Then Celtic drew breath, equalised two minutes after half time and, as right-winger Jimmy Johnstone led their rampage, Gary Sprake was injured in a collision with John Hughes. No sooner had David Harvey taken

Sprake's place in goal than he was beaten by a Bobby Murdoch shot that clinched Celtic's victory.

What greater ordeal could they face? Only a sadist might have scripted the manner of Leeds' extra-time defeat against Chelsea in the Cup final replay a fortnight later, a match that Leeds had again dominated, yet contrived to lose by two goals to one. Chelsea, who in Revie's words "had been murdered" during the Wembley game, were nothing if not durable though some of their defending had been primitive. "Robbery with Violence", one tabloid newspaper headline screamed the following day, Hardly anyone could believe it, not Revie, nor his players, nor the tearful Leeds supporters. Brian Clough, appearing as television pundit before the days that Leeds and Revie were to incur his habitual displeasure, clearly grieved for them and told the nation: "They have made the season." For the first time in recent history, Revie's warriors were gaining popular sympathy. They were making friends even. But, it seemed, they could not achieve all that and win things at the same time.

The stresses on the players had been immense. The loss of Paul Reaney, who broke his leg on 2 April in an away game at West Ham after Revie had decided not to pursue the championship, was the worst of many disruptive injuries. Never did the side have quite the settled look of the previous season, even before Revie's end-of-term experimental with reserves. The following campaign would be the greatest test of Revie's players' spirit and morale.

Chapter Eight

T HE LONG SLOG of the two previous seasons had brought Revie personal accolades. As well as his OBE, he had been voted Manager of the Year twice in succession. With his second award came the self-deprecation that some found praiseworthy and others distrusted. On receiving the 1970 award, the Leeds manager proclaimed: "If this award had been open to Britain, and the Scottish FA had the good sense to let their own managers be nominated . . . the Manager of the Year would certainly have been Jock Stein of Celtic."

Indeed, immediately after the emotionally charged defeats by Celtic in the European Cup, whatever grief may have been inside him Revie repressed in the name of good manners. He bestowed effusive praise on the Glasgow side and, Lord Harewood recalls, when a Leeds fan ventured to console him by suggesting that Celtic had been lucky Revie snapped back: "That wasn't bad luck. We were beaten by a great team."

The idea of courting the press and public opinion was, to some extent, instigated by Harry Reynolds yet it was instinctive in Revie too. That he was anxious to be liked, even as his sides were kicking lumps out of their opponents, was beyond doubt. Len Shackleton, who was briefly a team-mate of Revie at Sunderland before retiring and entering sports journalism, takes a sceptic's view of the Leeds manager's nice-guy image. "When it came to being elected Footballer of the Year in 1955 for instance, he set his stall out. It was calculated: he would be as nice as pie to the sports writers who might vote for him," Shackleton says.

Revie's deeds were, once again, to make him the target of another club, this time First Division rivals Birmingham City who offered a £100,000 contract. But as the Leeds manager had signed on for seven more years at Elland Road, the directors moved swiftly to rebut Birmingham's interest. And the gross disappointments of the previous season sharpened Revie's keenness once again to fulfil his ambitions with the fine side he had created. At Birmingham lay the unknown and the possibility of an indefinite wait for honours.

While the trials of 1969-70 would not be repeated, Revie's side was still to face some exquisitely savage reverses as it galloped away in indefatigable pursuit of every available trophy. It was also the season Revie would be driven beyond endurance to public condemnation of referee Mr Raymond Tinkler, of whom he had fallen foul six years earlier when he sought to persuade the official not to record his caution of Billy Bremner.

Any suggestion that the side might be at all battle-weary was dispelled in Leeds' opening salvo of five successive victories, achieved with a combination of great skill and cold-blooded efficiency. The momentum was temporarily halted by Arsenal, with whom Leeds drew in an old-style bruising encounter at Highbury. Yet soon they resumed their steady accretion of points, by now a habit, and save for an aberrational 3-0 defeat at Stoke City, the side remained unbeaten for almost four months before surrendering at Elland Road to Tottenham on 9 January. Interest in the League Cup had been relinquished early, perhaps gratefully, to Sheffield United in a 1-0 defeat, but Leeds' remorseless progress in Europe continued as the obscure and the powerful in turn were made light of. Competition in the Fairs Cup had become almost old hat to the Leeds supporters, and the likes of Sarpsborg, Dynamo Dresden, Sparta Prague and Vitoria Setubal all drew fewer than 30,000 spectators to Elland Road. Johnny Giles noted the somewhat blasé attitude of fans at this time. "They went around saying they'd wait until we got to the semi-finals," he recalls.

The tentative attitude of Leeds fans maddened Revie. He needed them in vast numbers to complete the fulfilment of his great dream: to create a great side, a winning side, a team both feared and loved, one that played constantly to packed houses as did Manchester United. He looked longingly and enviously at the crowds that flocked to Old Trafford; indeed, it was his obsession that Leeds should be bracketed with the club that Sir Matt Busby had created. "I want Leeds to be able to match Manchester United on all counts . . . to have won everything in sight; to be a magnetic drawing card wherever and whenever we play . . . in fact, I want us to be even better than anyone else," he said. But there must have been times that he felt Leeds United would remain forever excluded from Europe's élite as he surveyed, on gloomy nights, a half-full Elland Road that fell far short of being one of European soccer's great theatres.

But for prime fixtures Revie could expect 35-40,000, particularly as his side established its now familiar mid-season domination of the First Division. Again though, injuries conspired against him. He had been without Reaney until late November. In the crucial latter stages, he was to be lacking Bremner. Eddie Gray played fitfully throughout the season, recording just 18 League appearances. While Revie had strength in his reserves, notably the versatile and accomplished Mick Bates, there were times when the side found it hard to sustain form, having been deprived of two such creative players.

If, as Lord Harewood feels, Revie's Achilles heel was attracting more than his fair share of bad luck, occasionally his team would deny itself glory by atypical, inept performances. Revie's hunger for the FA Cup was unassuaged, and Leeds had progressed to the fifth round, disposing of Rotherham United, stubborn opponents who were only shifted after a replay, and, again, Swindon Town, before being drawn away to Colchester United, a modest Fourth Division team with, as Winston Churchill might have said, a great deal to be modest about. But at the end of their match at Layer Road, Leeds found themselves dumped uncomprehendingly out of the FA Cup, and an unwelcome legend had been created. Their 3-2 defeat was the greatest shock since Walsall had beaten the mighty Arsenal in 1933;

certainly no feat of giant-killing has since surpassed it in the public imagination.

It was not for the want of preparation. Revie had done his usual surveillance job, having had Colchester watched twice, and alerted his side to all the possible dangers. But he could not legislate for a series of defensive gaffes nor his team's unwillingness to hustle and harry in Fourth Division style. By the time his men had stepped up their game, it was too late; they were 3-0 down, and out. In the League, though, they responded in typical manner, winning their next four matches.

But Revie was not to win a championship race in which Leeds had been so dominant. It was not so much a buckling under the sheer pressure of fixtures, though the season had been no easy ride; it was more that Leeds' efforts were undone by a combination of the freakish and the phenomenal. The phenomenon was the grinding consistency of Arsenal, their principal challengers who, on the last lap, developed an extraordinary habit of winning games by a single late goal and so constantly nagged away at Leeds' lead.

On 17 April, showing some signs of end of season jitters, Leeds played West Bromwich at Elland Road. Here, their composure was undone by some grotesque refereeing by Ray Tinkler. Leeds were already 1-0 down and fighting to stay in the match when a misplaced pass by Norman Hunter bounced off Albion's Tony Brown. As Brown embarked on an optimistic chase towards the Leeds goal, linesman Bill Troupe raised his flag for offside against Colin Suggett who was several yards ahead of play. Brown stopped; all the Leeds players stopped, until Tinkler, to the astonishment of all, waved play on. Brown, almost diffidently, continued his journey towards Sprake's goal before squaring the ball to Jeff Astle whose sidefoot shot made it 2-0. For Leeds the match was now irretrievable.

Millions watching television witnessed Revie's rage and despair. The sense of menace at Elland Road was intense; but this was not the posturing, manufactured rage generated by gangs of penned hooligans. The pitch invasion, if that it may be called, was quite spontaneous and involved a handful of unconnected spectators from various parts of the ground, among them middle-aged men. "Tinkler," Revie said, "ruined nine months of hard work. At 1-0 down, Leeds were fighting back and Albion starting to crack." For

Revie and the Elland Road faithful, Ray Tinkler's decision was one disappointment too many. It defeated the Leeds manager's oft-practised self-control. But losing against West Bromwich was not, in itself, the end. Arsenal came to Elland Road and were beaten during a turbulent finale in which there was another offside furore. This time Leeds were the beneficiaries as referee Norman Burtenshaw allowed Jack Charlton's late goal. But Arsenal's knack of scraping late 1-0 victories had deserted them only temporarily. In their final match they defeated North London rivals Tottenham at White Hart Lane to secure the title.

Victory for Revie in the Fairs Cup, following forceful, intelligent performances against Liverpool, whom they beat 1-0 over a two-legged semi-final, and Juventus, in the final with whom they drew 3-3 on aggregate but conquered through the two goals scored in Turin, was a cause of satisfaction rather than euphoria, coming somewhat removed from the rest of the season on 3 June. When comparatively fresh Revie's players were much more able to assert their excellence and at least secure one trophy for their omnivorous manger.

While Revie was to attain most of his ambitions, trophies and glory rarely came to him in the grand, sweeping manner he longed for. The League Cup, that first elusive pot so necessary for everyone's psychological welfare at Elland Road, was the fruit of a match of attrition. The League Championship was won, and greatly celebrated, yet the achievement had lacked something in style. The two European trophies were worthwhile but not dazzling successes. Around all that was won, save in 1968-69, most people recalled much more readily the things Revie's teams had lost. And often when Leeds were victorious the detractors persisted, much to Revie's exasperation.

The season 1971-72 saw one of Revie's great dreams fulfilled. At last Leeds United won the FA Cup. But never can the celebration of winning England's finest Cup tournament have been so subdued. For most teams it would have been the crowning glory but Leeds, typically, still faced one more endurance test – a League match at Wolverhampton where the stakes were immense. Wolves stood between Leeds and the League and Cup double.

Leeds would not quite hit the consistent form that earned them the wholly unwanted record of having the most points ever, 64, for a team finishing runners-up. To start with, the FA had ordered them to play their first four home games on neutral grounds as punishment for the crowd trouble against West Bromwich. Their start was subdued. But playing with increasingly less inhibition, the team hit a patch of form early in 1972 so magnificent it would never be forgotten, and it brought Revie more than a fragment of joy. For whatever happened afterwards, he could never be accused of lacking a sense of soccer aestheticism. Millions watching on television were, once again, his witnesses as in rapid succession Manchester United, Southampton and Tottenham spun away from Elland Road in a daze, outplayed in a way they could not have imagined. The 5-1 defeat on 19 February of Revie's model club was merely a prelude to the extravagant 7-0 humiliation of Southampton two weeks later, a performance which Leeds might have been saving up for years to avenge the critics. The mocking keep-ball game, involving almost 30 consecutive passes, was described by one commentator as sadistic destruction.

Perhaps finest was the display against Tottenham in the FA Cup sixth round, although the winning margin was more modest, 2-1. For Revie, the 90 minutes and the headlines that followed the next day, momentarily made the previous 11 years seem worthwhile. "Leeds do their 'Real Thing'," said the *Observer*. Half a dozen world-class saves by Pat Jennings, who afterwards described Leeds as the best club side he had ever known, stood between Spurs and a rout. In the *Observer* report, Hugh McIlvanney described Leeds' football as "breathtaking in its scope and fluency, alive with dazzling improvisations . . . the full intimidating depth of their quality was never more manifest than in those early minutes. There was scarcely a weakness to be seen and excellence was everywhere." Beforehand, Revie's men had taken their place in a rather stagey, continental-style warm-up. The Leeds manager was going for glamour and, as long as the team sustained its performances, the decorative little pre-match rituals would be saved from bathos and ridicule.

Yet soon, Revie would be brought down to earth. Leeds' League form was not quite as consistent as in the previous year. He was to have a further argument with the trenchant Alan Hardaker over a fixture pile-up, for which, Hardaker claimed, Revie was once again to blame. Hardaker says that an out-of-form Newcastle offered to play Leeds the day after a ban on floodlit games caused by the three-day week and a national need to conserve energy ended. But when Hardaker passed on the offer, Revie declined on the grounds that Leeds never played on a Thursday. The game eventually took place on 19 April by which time Leeds' season was once more becoming highly pressurised. Newcastle, by then in much better shape, won 1-0. Those looking back with the wisdom of hindsight as to why the Championship was lost might also cite a match on 13 November at Southampton, which Leeds dominated but lost 2-1, and in which Revie had been without Clarke and Jones who were both unfit.

At the beginning of November Revie, conscious of the need to cover his key midfield players had sought to buy Asa Hartford from West Bromwich Albion. Hartford, a tenacious, dashing, attacking midfielder was the type of player Revie loved. But the deal, subject to the normal rigorous Elland Road medical, collapsed when it was revealed Hartford had a heart defect. (It did not, however, prevent Hartford from pursuing his vigorous career. Had Revie been unlucky? Or over-cautious?)

In the FA Cup, the virtuosity Leeds had shown was a springboard for passage to the final – Second Division Birmingham had been almost a soft touch as they were beaten 3-0 in the semi – and victory over Arsenal. In the week beforehand, Revie said: "If we do the double, I think we should not be classed as on a par with Real Madrid but just as Leeds United." He also mused on the way that the public now saw Leeds and their opponents. Arsenal, he said, were the good professional outfit only interested in getting results. Meanwhile, Elland Road was, at last acquiring the aura belonging to a great club. "I sensed it for the first time in the last few matches. You can feel the buzz beforehand . . . the electricity right throughout the crowd," Revie said.

It was a grand occasion, the centenary final, played on 6 May 1972, attended by the Queen and, at last, Leeds fans in raucous, passionate throngs. But the victory was less noble, a scuffling, bad-tempered game, above which Leeds could rise only fitfully after Allan Clarke's headed goal on the hour gave them the lead and the Cup for the first time in their history.

And so to Wolverhampton, for a match on which hung more than any in Revie's career. An approach to Alan Hardaker for rescheduling was, again, rejected, this time on the grounds that England's commitments against West Germany in the European Nations Cup and Wolves' own commitments against Tottenham in the UEFA Cup had left the League Management Committee no room for manoeuvre. Many professionals in the game were horrified that Leeds had so little respite after the Cup final following which there had been none of the traditional extravagant players' celebrations.

A draw at Wolverhampton was all Revie needed. Derby were top, having played all 42 matches. Leeds were second, with 57. Manchester City also had 57 but their programme was complete. Liverpool had 56 points from 41 matches.

It was a match the reverberations of which lasted for years. On the night, Wolves played with terrific fire and verve. Leeds, without Mick Jones, who had injured his elbow during the final against Arsenal, drafted in Mick Bates and played with matching fervour although Clarke and Giles were well below match fitness. When Wolves went 2-0 up by the 67th minute recovery was asking a little too much of Revie's team, even though Bremner, leading the attack, was driving them on like a demon and they pulled back a goal almost immediately.

Pity Revie. His side had given everything but found Parkes, the Wolves goalkeeper, in magnificent form, along with the rest of his team-mates. Afterwards, the distraught Leeds manager said: "It's just too much. We should have had at least three penalties. When you get decisions like that going against you, what can you do?" It was probably of small comfort to know that most of the rest of the football world agreed with him, though none denied the exhilarating contribution Wolves had made.

It was some months later before the match returned to haunt Revie, the subject of another in the anthology of matches the Leeds manager had allegedly sought to fix. The first allegations were made by the *Sunday People*, where three players claimed they had been approached and bribed with offers of up to £1,000 to help "throw" the match, to "take it easy". The FA investigated along with CID; inconclusively, but the scandal was revived five years later in the *Daily Mirror*'s trawl of matches in which, it was claimed, Revie's hand had attempted to pervert the course of football.

The *Mirror*'s story claimed to have the names, the missing links, that the *People* story had lacked. It was alleged that Mike O'Grady, the former Leeds winger, still with Wolves but on loan to Birmingham, had been approached by Revie as an intermediary to see if the Wolves players might be bribed so that the game would go in Leeds favour. The *Mirror* article, quite explicitly, had O'Grady claiming that Revie made the offer, and O'Grady made the approach on his behalf. The interview then carried a strong flavour of O'Grady's subsequent unease about his remarks. He does not deny speaking to the newspaper. "They chased me and I spoke to them. At the time I didn't think very highly of Revie after the England episode" (Revie's later defection from management of England to manage the United Arab Emirates). But O'Grady rejects all the allegations attributed to him. "Though I didn't go to my solicitor because I was very upset about it all," he says.

The *Daily Mirror* was keen to hike up its saga in the wake of the *Daily Mail*, which had carried the incontrovertible scoop about Revie's defection from the England job and his clandestine dealings with United Arab Emirates. But some stories showed signs of being loosely stitched together and, where names are named, they usually relate to players who merely admit to being approached. Theirs was no disgrace.

From the Leeds point of view, Peter Lorimer's reflections are interesting. "If the boss tried to fix anything, we never saw it," he says. "I've never really seen it in the game. There used to be the odd joke if we were playing a team last game of the season and we needed the points and they were in mid-table. If you had some of your Scottish pals playing, you'd say: 'Hope you're not going to have a real go today.' You'd say that in general. You'd say: 'Hope you're going to take it easy on us.' But if you're talking about us going up to one of them with a couple of hundred quid to say 'You're not going to have a go today' . . . then I've never seen that. But we all used to do it jokingly. I remember saying to big Franny Munro, who was a pal of mine, that night: 'I hope you're not going to kick us around.' That was just a bit of banter. But if you were trying to put a story together, people could say they were trying to say something. I was a pal of Franny . . . I said it as a joke. Wolves played out of their skins that night . . . perhaps because of a bit of hatred of Leeds. They wouldn't have played like that normally. But I don't know if an approach was made that night, I'll be a hundred per cent honest."

In the *Mirror* article, Munro's name was mentioned as one of those approached. But he couldn't give any names. Lorimer points out that actually to get a match fixed would take considerable effort. "If you got to one or two players, the other nine, in a good team, could still carry the match. And you would certainly have to go for the goalkeeper." Of the whole opaque business few things are sure, save that years later Gary Sprake told a court he was paid £15,000 by the *Mirror* for his series of allegations against Revie (the substance of which he subsequently denied), and that when the *People* were, in another article rash enough to implicate Billy Bremner, he sued, and won £100,000 in libel damages. Such were the waves created by that hectic night at Wolverhampton.

The 1972-73 season opened with a 4-0 defeat at Chelsea, Leeds' heaviest first-day loss for 24 years. But all was not as it seemed. With Hunter and Clarke suspended, and Peter Lorimer deputising in goal for the injured David Harvey, who had finally ousted Gary Sprake after seven years waiting in the wings, predictions that Revie's side was about to disintegrate were wildly premature. They were, however now functioning with one enforced change. Terry Cooper had broken his leg in the 3-0 away victory against Stoke City in April, robbing Leeds of a player with exciting and varied skills. As a small job-lot, Revie had brought to Elland Road defenders Trevor Cherry and Roy Ellam from Huddersfield; and such was the structural soundness of the defensive operation created by Revie that Cherry, though a less exciting player than Cooper, proved a sturdy replacement.

The Chelsea aberration was followed by swift recovery and the inevitable charge up the table. But suspensions and injuries meant that Leeds would not dominate affairs as completely as in some previous seasons. Jack Charlton, now 37, would appear only fitfully and retire from the club at the end of the season to manage Middlesbrough, after 20 years service at Elland Road. He would eventually be replaced by the massive frame of Gordon McQueen, bought from St Mirren that September and eased by Revie into Charlton's slot as the season ended. Another young Scot, Joe Jordan, a front-man with a marauding style of play whom Revie had acquired from Morton two years earlier, was also drafted in for the injured Mick Jones. But enforced disruptions undermined consistency, though the sheer habit of winning, as ever, sustained Leeds almost to the last on all fronts, save in the League Cup.

In the end, all that, and much more, would be overshadowed by another excruciating finale to the season, containing all the old ingredients: wicked luck, grotesque refereeing, the mysterious abandonment of form that afflicted Leeds in their hours of greatest need. After the débâcle against Colchester in the FA Cup two seasons earlier, few would have bet that Leeds might, once again, be ripe for a second public humiliation of such proportions in the same competition. This time, it would be at Wembley, in the final, against Sunderland, for whose chances no one outside the buoyant Wearside city gave a candle. Sunderland, managed by Bob Stokoe, the man who probably despised Revie more than any other in football.

There had been few confrontations between them since Leeds' relegation struggle against Bury 11 years before. Sunderland came to Wembley in the highest of spirits; commentators and television viewers on the match day were struck by the contrasting exuberance of Stokoe's men compared with the rigid, uneasy air that surrounded Revie and his team. Stokoe had already been conducting some psychological warfare beforehand. He had always taken exception to the manner in which he felt Leeds players in general, and Billy Bremner especially, harassed referees. So Stokoe announced to the media the previous Wednesday: "Ken Burns [the Cup final referee] won't allow that." The Sunderland manager says drily: "I was very satisfied. He had a tremendous game." As part of his campaign, he also complained about Leeds having the pick of the Wembley dressing-rooms and the choice of the best end for their supporters.

For Stokoe, perhaps the only blight on his greatest day was a television link-up interview with Revie during which the demands of the media required him to produce a phoney bonhomie. Peter Lorimer has a vivid memory of Revie's highly-strung state that day. "Eddie Gray and I were going downstairs in our hotel. There was a photographer at the bottom and he took a picture of us. Don grabbed the camera off him and nearly threw it through the window. He didn't like pictures of his team being taken before the games. It was his own personal superstition."

So many curious memories surround the doings of Revie's Leeds. It is probably the only Cup final where the single goal that won it was overshadowed by a non-goal – the astounding save that Sunderland goalkeeper Jim Montgomery made to deny Peter Lorimer an equaliser as Leeds applied incessant pressure on the Sunderland penalty area. A goal might have been applauded by only 20,000 out of 100,000 fans. Sunderland, too, had been allocated 20,000 tickets but appeared to have the support of almost all the 60,000 neutrals. After the final, Revie delivered his knee-jerk congratulations to the victorious manager, distress etched into his face. Stokoe had never been so exultant, but even in victory found the opportunity to mock Revie in front of the television cameras. Flouting Cup final dress convention by wearing a red track suit, he said: "I hadn't a lucky suit like Don Revie so I decided I'd come as one of the lads."

Whither the Leeds manger? At last, it was reported, he had received an offer he could not refuse, to become manager of Everton, a side in steady decline from their League Championship form of three seasons earlier. The reports came as Leeds, yet again, were in post-season pursuit of European glory; for neither injuries nor suspensions had arrested the impetus that inevitably led them to the crux of one European contest or another. But as they arrived on Greek soil in Salonika to battle with AC Milan in the European Cup Winners Cup final, Revie's 12-year reign seemed about to end. With Clarke and Bremner suspended, Giles and Gray injured, Cooper still absent with his broken leg, the roars of Sunderland fans possibly still echoing in their ears, Leeds, for once, entered neither as favourites nor with high morale. The match was, in a way, to encapsulate Revie's era at Leeds, and was largely undone for them by the roguishness of the Greek referee, Christos Michas, whom UEFA had felt fit to put in charge despite the fact that the previous year he had been banned from refereeing for three months after an outrageously aberrant display during a League game between two Greek teams.

Never again would Mr Michas be allowed control of a match of any importance. After four minutes, an apparently honest tackle by Paul Madeley near the Leeds area was penalised. The resulting indirect free kick took a deflection and beat Harvey.

The remaining 86 minutes were a wretched tale of Milan, aided and abetted by the referee, surviving almost constant Leeds pressure. The neutral Greeks in the crowd sided with Leeds as three legitimate penalty claims were denied Revie's team. Two minutes from the end, Norman Hunter could take no more, and was sent off for retaliating in the face of constant and vicious fouls by the Milanese. It was a match in which Leeds won nothing but sympathy. By now, Revie was a connoisseur of defeat, the flavour of this one tasting not unlike the one in 1970, when Chelsea and the FA Cup final replay had been the ingredients.

At home, Everton, a lucrative contract and a chance to escape the pain still awaited. But so did complications; the obstructive deliberations of the Leeds board, the possibility of any deal that was too munificent being referred to a government pay board. Meanwhile, journalists wrote their obituaries. One said: "Revie . . . realises his players can do no more for him . . . he surely recognises his ship needs a refit and, after it a new ship's company." Many believed the breaker's yard beckoned for his great but unfulfilled team. How wrong the many were to be.

Chapter Nine

THE GOOD NEWS came from Greece; the only cheer Leeds fans extracted from their miserable expedition. Revie was staying. His reasons were opaque, encapsulated in the word "personal", a convenient expression that explains little or nothing. Everton, like other clubs offered to him beforehand, could take some salvaging. Within Leeds, he was revered; outside, less so. His ship would remain afloat after all, the company the same; but there was some brushing up to be done.

The acclamation of Leeds' brilliant performances had in part given way once again to public condemnation. The 1972-73 season had been bad for discipline. A procession of Revie's players had made trips to disciplinary hearings to contest bookings. By March, Norman Hunter and Trevor Cherry had collected eight each. There had been many gruelling encounters, not least the away fixture at Derby County on 3 March, won by Leeds 3-2, which caused further inflammatory utterances by Brian Clough against Revie, his team and all its works. (There was now no greater critic of Leeds than Clough who, two months earlier, had offended guests when speaking at a dinner in Peter Lorimer's honour, accusing the Leeds forward of falling over when he had not been kicked and protesting when he had nothing to protest about.)

The season had ended with the FA imposing a £3,000 fine on Revie's team, to be suspended only if the club cleaned up its act. The new one was preceded by a set-piece public relations exercise. Revie called a press conference at which he promised better behaviour and, moreover, asked for everyone's help in achieving the objective, from the FA to the press. To help make the side more lovable, the club had appointed its first public relations officer, Peter Fay, a man in his twenties with many good ideas about how to make visits to Elland Road more agreeable. The practice of kicking plastic footballs into the crowd and giving away the fancy little stocking tags, begun during the previous season, would continue. Meanwhile, at the press conference, Revie avoided the trap of turning on his audience, and, as he had done in the past, of suggesting Leeds had been persecuted by the media. He also eschewed mention of Brian Clough, of whom he had said: "If all the managers and players acted like him, knocking each other all the time, then there very soon wouldn't be any game left." In his latest outburst, Clough had suggested Leeds should be demoted to the Second Division as punishment for their antics.

The same ageing group of players whose demise had been so widely predicted would serve him once again. One departure, though, was Gary Sprake who could not find a way back into the first team. Again Revie's dealings with him seemed not quite straight. "I wanted regular first-team football and had signed a three-year contract with a three-year option. I don't think he wanted me to go, though he said, 'If you say you want to go, that is up to you.' A testimonial was never mentioned . . . but I never got one after playing for the club for 13 years," Sprake says.

He departed for Birmingham City, his lack of a money-spinning testimonial a sore point, though not something on which he chooses to dwell now. Yet despite his odd treatment of Sprake, Revie still wanted to be friends. He had a habit of sending his players telegrams of congratulations whenever they played an international match. Sprake had received 44 of them, following his appearances in goal for Wales at various levels. At Birmingham, he continued receiving solicitous telegrams from Revie while in hospital undergoing a series of painful back operations on injuries that eventually forced him out of football.

Already at something of a distance from Revie's "family", Sprake's association with the *Daily Mirror* bribes stories caused him to be ostracised by almost all except Paul Reaney. Mention Sprake's name to the likes of Giles and Hunter and they bridle, believing he was an agent through whom some of Leeds' finest deeds, for which they had sweated, were devalued. "Give Johnny my regards. I'd like to see his face," Sprake said. When these were passed on, Giles's face barely moved a muscle and he carried on speaking, as if he had not heard.

The recuperative powers of Leeds' players, both physical and psychological, were never more evident than at the start of 1973-74. Once more Revie had managed to fire them up, though he could hardly have wished for a more self-motivated squad. Sharp, intensive training had made them match fit from the off. Revie had promised the world best behaviour and clean, attacking football. Yet the last price he would dream of paying was forfeiture of success.

Perhaps only the most faithful might have been prepared for the virtuosity with which Revie's team opened its campaign. The ageing team that some had written off struck form that rekindled memories of 18 months earlier when merely workmanlike opposition was just swept aside. The doctrine of attack and better discipline was put into immediate practice in the 3-1 defeat of Everton as the season opened. Three days later, Revie's team found the wit and craft to win 2-1 at Arsenal after being a goal behind. Leeds returned to North London, to Tottenham, for their next match, and here served notice that no one in the First Division might be able to match them. Neither in defence nor attack did Tottenham have any answer to the fluid, persistent play that brought Leeds a 3-0 victory.

Revie's dream of creating the team of ultimate football aesthetes from his collection of once-ugly ducklings was again in full bloom. As they notched up their seventh successive victory at Southampton, John Arlott recorded in *The Guardian*: "Wearing the white strip of a blameless life, Leeds moved in a ceaseless flow, back in packed defence, competing for the midfield, sweeping forward and with backs overlapping. Yet it was all so controlled, almost amiable . . ." Only in the next match did the first blemishes appear on this record of perfection: a point dropped at home in a goal-less draw with Manchester United; a booking against Joe Jordan for retaliating against one in a series of savage challenges.

One of Peter Fay's innovations was to beef up the club programme which hitherto had been a dismal product, unworthy of a club with aspirations to greatness. Into it, for the first time, Revie poured his thoughts. It was a splendid public relations opportunity. His notes preceding the home game against Wolverhampton Wanderers condemned 'knocking' of the game by other managers. "Stop this constant bickering and sniping. It serves no constructive purpose whatsoever . . . I am slowly sinking in a surfeit of bad publicity. All I seem to read on the back pages is how bad the game is." Revie the reformer appealed for press reports to highlight the constructive elements of the game which his own team was displaying in abundance. Points for goals, cried Revie on another occasion, as his forwards popped them in one after another; and patience from directors, who should give their managers a fair crack of the whip. More than once Revie would campaign on his hobby horse of Sunday football, first articulated almost 20 years earlier in his Manchester City days. The possibility of increased attendances – always one of Revie's obsessions – was his principal argument. "I think it is time to consider a permanent change to Sunday soccer in the Summer and with a mid-Winter break." When it came to a conflict between God and football, football won. "I appreciate the Lord's Day Observance Society would have great cause for complaint. But football, remember, is our national sport . . . a pastime as vital to our social pattern as any other industry," Revie said.

By 11 November, as Leeds had gone 15 matches unbeaten and it looked to the rest of the League as if they might disappear over the horizon, Revie was publicly contemplating the possibility of his side going undefeated all season. Peter Lorimer recalls the intensity of Revie's ambition around this time. "We played a home game in which we drew and didn't play particularly well. But the boss was determined we were going to win the League. He read the riot act to us after that match, tore into us, telling us what we were doing and what we weren't doing. I think the lads were a bit shocked he came on so strong. But he had had so many disappointments . . . he probably wanted to make sure we would win it that season."

Victories by 3-0 at home to Coventry on 17 November and at Ipswich on 8 December brought more plaudits for the elegance with which they were achieved. Christmas came and went, with Leeds still unbeaten. Beforehand, on 15 December, they had overhauled Liverpool's record of 19 unbeaten matches from the beginning of a season with a 2-1 victory against Chelsea at Stamford Bridge. On 29 December their standard was three minutes from falling, at Birmingham City, until a late break and cross by Lorimer enabled Jordan to score the goal that saved the day.

Unlike in 1968-69, Revie's team was being consistently disrupted by injuries. Leeds would be much of the season without Giles, source of so many of their most intelligent moves. Once again, Eddie Gray would miss most of a season, playing just one game after the bruising September encounter with Manchester United. Injuries also bedevilled Mick Jones but in Jordan Revie had a more than adequate substitute. The quality of reserves, such as Mick Bates, who had so often deputised with distinction for Giles, and Terry Yorath, less creative but a warrior, was crucial in sustaining the side, as was the seemingly infinite versatility of Paul Madeley, provider of strength and variety in midfield, and the speed with which Gordon McQueen learned his job so soon after Jack Charlton's departure.

The unbeaten record was, however, growing burdensome. Leeds had shuffled off the distraction of the League Cup at the first hurdle, losing 2-0 to Ipswich in October and, by December, had departed the UEFA Cup, losing 3-2 on aggregate to Vitoria Setubal. The home game had attracted just 14,196 to Elland Road, a clear indication of where supporters', if not Revie's, priorities lay. But as January and February passed, every League match had the intensity of a Cup tie. "Teams would improve their game 70-80 per cent against us," says Peter Lorimer. Indications that cracks were about to appear came in the FA Cup when, after a 1-1 draw, Leeds lost to Bristol City 1-0 in the FA Cup fifth round replay. Again, even in defeat, Revie was ever mindful of niceties. The referee for both matches had been Jack Taylor. "In the first game, Revie had been moaning about decisions which had gone against him," Taylor recalls. "But after they lost at Elland Road, he came in and said I had had a great game."

Leeds' proud run in the League toppled just four days later. The manner of their defeat at Stoke City had horrible echoes of past disasters. Already without Jones, McQueen and Reaney, a 19th minute groin injury to Johnny Giles, when Leeds were already two goals up, proved impossible to assimilate. Cooper, recently returned after 21 months following his broken leg, was not, on this occasion, the man to fill Giles' role. By the 67th minute, Leeds were 3-2 down, Bremner and Clarke were booked and Leeds players' tempers had frayed to the extent that they plunged into intense recriminations with referee John Homewood. It was not, of course, the end of everything; they still had an eight-point lead, as Revie and all commentators were swift to point out. But dreadful doubts bubbled under the surface. The 1-0 away defeat by Liverpool on 15 March began an excruciating run of three successive failures. The 4-1 home defeat by Burnley and the 3-1 loss at West Ham showed every indication that Revie's pre-season emphasis on style and accent on discipline had been jettisoned as the Merseyside club stalked remorselessly, scenting the possibility of spectacular collapse.

As April arrived, Revie was crying out for three points for an away victory. His side was performing almost as well on its travels as at Elland Road. Three points for an away win – Leeds had won ten times on their travels – would have made their position, now precarious, impregnable. Liverpool had only four away victories! Revie also called out for professional referees. "They might put a stop to an unsavoury tactic – that of trying deliberately to get opponents cautioned. Whether they feign injury after tackles or put on an act good enough to bring them an Oscar, it is all the same. It should stop – and stop now." There would have been some managers in the game, not least Brian Clough, who would have found Revie's homily a collectors' item among life's little ironies.

The home game against Derby, on 6 April, brought a 2-0 win and allowed some nerves to steady. Bremner, as so often when playing as an auxiliary striker, had inspired with his skill and his energy. But it was not a turning point. There were successive jittery, ill-tempered, goal-less draws against Coventry and Sheffield United over Easter. The day after playing at Elland

Road, Leeds were back at Bramall Lane. At half time, there was no score and news reached them that Liverpool had already scored four times against Manchester City at Anfield. Revie was on the threshold of his worst nightmare. Leeds redoubled their efforts, not least through Mick Jones, playing with an injured knee, but Peter Lorimer was to be the saviour. Two goals from him, the second a penalty, brought a priceless victory. The 3-2 defeat of Ipswich four days later, a match in which nerves were strained almost beyond endurance, was to be conclusive, though no one realised it at the time. Liverpool, five points behind, though with two games in hand, had struck their own patch of inconsistent form. In their penultimate game, at home to Arsenal, they lost 1-0. Revie had transported himself out of the family home to a friend's house. "Every time I do that, I get the right result and it has worked again," he said. And as he sipped champagne, it was as much to celebrate his relief as his championship triumph.

Chapter Ten

I MMEDIATE TALK was of the following season, the European Cup and any other prize that might be on offer. But things were different for Revie now. At the end of 1972-73, there had been much to put right; a savage sense of loss, a dreadful disciplinary record which gave Leeds such a poor image. Revie would not have wished to depart Elland Road in failure, the subject of obloquy. He liked nice endings. However insatiable he declared his ambition to be, 1974 had at last brought the richest domestic prize, confounding the commentators who felt it was beyond his squad of ageing players.

And now there was a job in the wind that was to prove irresistible. Perhaps doubts, his perennial over-caution, a feeling he might, as he always did, get a better deal from Leeds in the end, had failed to lure Revie to Torino, Birmingham and Everton. But the chance to manage England was another matter; for a man of serious ambition, an opportunity that could not be spurned. Moreover, the squad of players described as ageing at the end of the previous season were a year older again. How might Revie face dismantling the squad he had nurtured over 13

116

years? Whatever his managerial skills, they were not at their best when it came to getting rid of players. Lord Harewood recalls: "The team was all the same age. The agony of having to replace them was something he was glad not to face. He said that it was a fundamental reason for him leaving. Yet leaving was agony too . . . could he bear to leave what he had built up?"

But as the English caretaker managership of Joe Mercer was coming to a close Revie contacted Ted Croker, the FA secretary, with his declaration of interest. Croker sat up at once. Here was the man with the best club record in England; it was improbable a candidate of higher calibre would be found. Croker, who had moved into his job the previous season, had fresh in his mind the reformed Leeds of those early months. "I remember their match against Chelsea (the match in which Leeds broke the First Division record of unbeaten matches from the start of a season). I saw Don Revie and Billy Bremner, and congratulated them, saying how delighted I was . . . not so much that they had broken the record but that they had had a complete change of heart."

Sir Andrew Stephen, the FA chairman, was similarly enthusiastic. Croker, he and Dick Wragg, chairman of the International Committee, dashed off to Elland Road for talks. They were impressed with Revie's personality and ideas. Little time was wasted. An appointment would take place immediately if the Leeds board accepted Revie's resignation and terms were settled. Things moved swiftly. The Leeds board accepted an offer of money to assist with the appointment of a new manager. Revie had flown and taken with him Les Cocker. An era in which so many emotions had been spilled ended, so it seemed, quite unsentimentally. Revie, so the Leeds board hoped, would remain until his successor was installed. But the day after his appointment had been announced, Revie had cleared his desk.

Of course, his spirit, his shadow, had not gone. He had done so much; though there were smaller things he had not done. He left in his wake a somewhat disillusioned Syd Owen, on whose efforts and constancy he had much depended. Owen recalls, with marked self-restraint: "I was disappointed that having been at the club all that time, having been a loyal servant to Don, having played a great part in the development of some of the players, he didn't give his staff the security in football he was looking for himself in the future . . . that he didn't make sure all the coaches and physios who had served him had been made more secure with contracts. I was at that club all those years and put in all those hours . . . but when I wrote a letter of resignation, all I got was what I had worked for. I understand Don had made a signed agreement that he would come back to the club as a consultant. Having done that, I would have thought he would also have looked after his loyal servants."

Owen's era at Elland Road was soon to be over. When, after the upheavals of succession, Jimmy Armfield eventually came to be installed as manager, Owen asked for a contract. "But he said he couldn't be of any help to me so I wrote a letter of resignation and just walked out," Owen says. He soon departed to Birmingham City, managed by one of his former charges Willie Bell, where it took the players a little time to get over the shock of Owen's rigorous demands in training. But Armfield's eventual succession was not what anybody had planned – not Revie nor the directors. Revie had recognised in Johnny Giles someone capable of succeeding him. "Don had great admiration for him as player . . . he was a kind of person who was always cool and calculated," says Owen. But the directors were not to take Revie's advice, not least because they felt disinclined to heed suggestions from the man who had abandoned them so swiftly for the England job.

As it happened, Giles was not hungry for the job. He had been in Germany watching the World Cup when he heard of Revie's departure. "I came back to see the boss because I wanted to get my contract sorted out. Then he told me he had recommended me for the job. He didn't say why . . . he didn't have to and I didn't ask him. But I was never bothered, never heartbroken."

However, Giles has little good to say about the Leeds directors who ignored Revie's advice. "They never appreciated the success they had. The directors said to themselves: 'This is the easiest game in the world.' The club was millions ahead and everything was a joyride. They hadn't been in the game long enough to know the downs as well as the ups. They should have hung on his every word but they thought, 'He's only a manager. If we advertise this job, we'll get a hundred people.' But you wouldn't have got a hundred Don Revies, that's for sure."

What they got instead was the singular Brian Clough, who blustered and blundered his way into the club which he had expended so much energy criticising, and who was to tell the players, at his first team talk, that they should throw away their medals and cups because they had all been won by cheating. It was tremendous slight, not only on them but on Revie, for whom all had sweated. Clough immediately and irredeemably offended Billy Bremner by ordering him to pay his own £500 fine after being sent off in a fracas with Kevin Keegan during the FA Charity Shield match against Liverpool at Wembley. In the past, Revie had seen to his players' disciplinary fines.

Earlier, the managerial position at Leeds had given Bremner himself something to mull over. Syd Owen recalls: "Manny Cussins, the chairman, had arranged to see Giles about Don's recommendation when Billy Bremner walked down the passage at about nine-fifteen in the morning. I had never seen Billy at the ground at that time before. He had come to tell Manny Cussins that he was interested in the vacancy as well." On this matter, Bremner himself is coy. "I remember seeing John in the foyer and saying, 'It looks as it you are going to get the job.' He said: 'We'll talk about that if it develops.' " But on the matter of approaching the Leeds directors himself, Bremner says: "I can't remember."

Revie might have departed but Owen was determined his high standards of professionalism should continue. There was an immediate clash of cultures in the Revie way and the Clough way. Owen recalls: "The first morning Clough came to the club as manager, he brought his two sons with him. I was just taking the reserves and the junior players out for training when he shouted to me down the corridor and asked me if I could get one of the apprentices to take his two boys into the gymnasium and entertain them while we were out. I told him the apprentices were here to develop their capabilities as professional footballers and not look after the manager's boys. I said: 'There are no groundstaff boys available. They are not here to entertain your children.' After that, I would just get on with my job and avoid him."

A minority had had misgivings about Revie's appointment as England manager. Two who expressed their feelings to Ted Croker were Alan Hardaker, who had told him and anyone at the FA who would listen that they needed their heads examining, and Croker's brother, Peter. Why? Croker says: "I thought Revie had cleaned up his act and that was why I was so keen on him. I think my brother felt that leopards don't change their spots . . . Revie had a reputation for developing very hard players." Hardaker's antipathy was well-known. But the dissenters were few. Most looked forward to the emergence of an English side after the traumas of the previous year and the 1-1 draw against Poland that had killed off hopes of qualifying for the World Cup.

Where should Revie begin? He might start with improving the public relations side of things, where there was much scope for image-making. Sir Alf Ramsey had not endeared himself to the media, not through any particular antipathy it had to him but because he did not feel compelled to sell himself. He had been polite but distant. Revie told the players that the press had a job to do, and that they should put themselves out to help. Drinks and sandwiches would be offered to reporters at press conferences. The tricks of management he had learned at the knee of Harry Reynolds were continuing. And some sort of a bond with the players should be formed too. Closeness and continuity had underpinned everything at Leeds.

So, soon after his appointment, Revie gathered no fewer than 81 current and potential England players for an overnight get together at a Manchester hotel. Ted Croker, in hindsight, feels it was a mistake. "Ultimately, it proved not to be a good idea . . . it gave players far too many delusions of grandeur before they'd actually done their donkey work of achieving a lot more success in the League. That represented four players per First Division club. You haven't got four players of international standard per club." But Mike Channon, who played more games under Revie than anyone else, considers the new manager was merely being professional. "He wanted to be able to call on everyone . . . but I think he took on a lot," he says.

Having effected his introductions, Revie turned his businesslike mind to other matters. The players had been told at the Manchester gathering that while the basic fee for an England appearance would remain at £100, there would now be a £100 bonus for a draw and £200 for a win. When Revie came later to be pilloried by the press, this move was to be held up by the more vituperative critics as an example of his obsession with money. But there was little outcry at the time.

Another commercial deal completed as the Revie era began was sponsorship of the England kit by the sportswear firm Admiral. The stern critics used it as a stick with which to beat Revie in later, more hostile times when they were after his blood. It is an often misunderstood transaction. Croker says: "It benefitted the FA, not the players. It was the first of the deals where somebody provided the kit and paid a premium on the basis of replica sales. I remember Admiral writing in . . . we got a quotation from them and another company. Don was very much on the fringe of things . . . I have no evidence whatsoever that he got anything out of the Admiral deal."

With a deft touch of populism, Revie decided to introduce *Land of Hope and Glory* as the team's anthem before matches. In fact he did everything in his power to create the perfect climate before his first international match against Czechoslovakia. But there had been some uncomfortable moments on the way, involving principally his old adversary Alan Hardaker. With him, Revie had explored the possibility of League fixtures being postponed the Saturday before important international games. Hardaker told him that to grant his request immediately was impossible for various reasons; not least because it could create the sort of fixture pile-up that had caused Revie himself so much grief as Leeds manager. But on the strength of Hardaker intimating that it might be reconsidered in the future, Revie appeared at a sports writers' lunch soon after and in a speech implied that Hardaker would go along with his wishes.

Hardaker was so indignant he issued a statement squashing any such notion. Yet he didn't want to be seen as sabotaging England's chances of playing the world's best with eleven fit players. Soon after, he and Revie had another lively meeting at Football League headquarters. This time the League secretary was in a constructive mood. An agreement was struck whereby Saturday fixtures near an international would be brought forward to Wednesday so that the England manager would have almost a week to try and get players to peak fitness. It was a qualified triumph for Revie's manipulative skills.

Despite Revie's peerless achievements at Leeds, Ted Croker was soon to make a discovery that disturbed him; namely that Revie had not qualified as an FA coach. While it seemed to have had a negligible effect on the fortunes of Leeds United, Croker says: "It was important in terms of giving credibility to the coaching scheme as such, although not so vitally important in terms of doing the job. Courses are useful because they bring managers together, if only to talk among themselves." It seemed almost as if some form of etiquette had been breached. Revie, as he was to find later, was now in strange surroundings.

Revie's managerial debut, the European Championship home match against Czechoslovakia in October 1974, was to produce another qualified triumph. A crowd of 86,000 turned up at Wembley, where they were issued with song sheets for *Land of Hope and Glory*. But for most of the match the occasion threatened anti-climax until, with the double substitution of Trevor Brooking and Dave Thomas for Martin Dobson and Frank Worthington, England found the penetration that had eluded them. Two minutes later, Channon scored from a Thomas cross and two more goals followed to bring Revie an unforeseen and gratifying 3-0 victory.

Under Ramsey, the players and all the England establishment had been used to a settled side. In ten years, there had been more stability within Leeds United than any other League club. It was to come as a surprise to almost everyone, then, that one of Revie's principal managerial characteristics during his England reign was a seemingly chronic inability to decide on his best team. A month later, in the match against Portugal at Wembley, four England players had lost their places. For the following match, also at Wembley, against West Germany, the side was again almost entirely reshuffled.

Croker began to feel uneasy about Revie's suitability for the job after all. "He was changing his mind all the time . . . it changed my whole outlook on the sort of person who was a good England manager. Alf Ramsey never asked a player to do a job he didn't do for his club. But Don, because he had had the tremendous success of playing one or two people in different roles – particularly Paul Madeley – rather got the impression he could do it at England level, that he could take the eleven best players in the country and make a team of them. But the time you have with players is so short that you can't vary much what they're doing at club level. Don had this sort of idea you could do the sort of things he did at Leeds with the England team and that just wasn't on."

Revie was too much a creature of habit to abandon the methods that had served him so well. With him came the dossiers and the pre-match get together rituals: enforced sessions of bingo and carpet bowls. On such innocent amusements he had weaned his

Leeds United family. But now he was dealing with less malleable material. If some England players lacked a particularly clear idea of what they did want to do with their time, they were fairly clear they did not want to play Revie's parlour games.

While Alan Ball would claim that Revie was afraid of independent spirits within the camp, Mike Channon is more sympathetic. "He wanted the England team to be his boys, like at Leeds. He would go, 'Come on, lads, we're having bowls tonight,' on a Friday night. But we were England! I think he was unfortunate to get it wrong. And I think once he fell out with someone, he couldn't forgive." In 13 years at Leeds, Revie had had to deal with only the minimum of recalcitrance among his players. England was proving a new and unpleasant experience for him. His pre-match ten o'clock curfew and his dossiers were often ignored. Channon says: "Of course we used to sneak out. I used to rebel against being told what do. You treat people like children and they behave like them."

It was a puzzle to many why Revie, who had stuck so long with his great Leeds players and often had them out to do battle when they were unfit, suddenly appeared to have no long-term design. At Leeds there had from the outset been a grand plan, a master strategy. But now he had no mentor: there was no Harry Reynolds to guide him. Yet still he liked to please, to be in the swim of public opinion. Ted Croker finds the contrast with Sir Alf Ramsey striking. "Alf judged a player by international appearances . . . after the previous game, barring one or two injuries, he knew what his team was going to be for the next game. I think that is one of the most important features of a manager's success . . . he must not respond to the public clamour you tend to get to try this new lad or that new lad. You will always lose out.

"But Don was completely different. After an international match, he would come in and have a chat about who had played well and who had played badly, and I could see his thoughts about the team. Then he would watch a game the next week and see one of those players who had played well or badly, and be influenced by that, or he'd see another player who had played exceptionally well in a team doing well and be extremely tempted to bring him in. There were constant changes going on. From that experience, I recommended to his successors, Ron Greenwood and Bobby

Robson, that the most important thing was to try and keep a settled team. You get player loyalty, too, that Don never really got at international level. Though the one thing I never did was to volunteer an opinion about team selection unless I was asked."

After a year of Revie's management, Croker's misgivings had become pronounced. "I didn't think he was getting as much out of the players as was available. It was as simple as that. I felt he was being distracted by commercial deals. And he just didn't have the players available to him . . . he was not happy about not having them directly under his control. It was frustrating to him. With Revie and Brian Clough, their success had been personal, based on the contact they had made with players. Revie had developed this father-figure image . . . he virtually controlled their lives. This is something that doesn't feature in international football. You have to survive from November . . . you don't play again until February – three months when the England manager doesn't have a player under his control. The people you rely on being a father-figure certainly aren't the sort you want for an England manager."

Revie's third match, with another rearranged side, was against West Germany and brought a 2-0 victory. He showed a neat managerial touch by the symbolic appointment as captain of Alan Ball, who was the sole survivor of England's 1966 World Cup victory. To ensure maximum pre-match publicity, Revie called a press conference to make the announcement. Asked if Ball's appointment would be permanent, Revie's answer was typically ambivalent. "That's entirely up to him." But it was a match that fulfilled the expectations of Revie, Ball and a critical public: a sweet, smooth performance in which Alan Hudson of Stoke City played an outstanding game in midfield.

Revie retained Ball as captain for the next five matches which, with more chopping and changing of players, included two victories against Cyprus and, in the Home Internationals, a goal-less draw in Belfast against Northern Ireland, a 2-2 draw with Wales at Wembley, and a 5-1 victory over Scotland which was possibly Revie's finest hour as England manager. It was a match in which Gerry Francis, returning to the side after injury, showed magnificent form, though he could not have expected that following it Ball would be jettisoned by Revie to make way for him as captain.

Revie's dealings with some senior players had already been uneasy. Before the match against Wales he had, with minimal explanation, told Emlyn Hughes that he would not be picked for the match and nor would he be needed in future. Hughes, still only 27 and a former captain, was dumbfounded. Yet it was typical of Revie's indecision as England manager that two years later, he would recall Hughes for the crucial World Cup qualifying match against Italy. Hughes had received advance warning of Revie's intentions from his Liverpool manager Bob Paisley, but when Revie telephoned he gave vent to the indignation that had been seething inside him for two years. In a second call soon after, Revie told Hughes he had changed his mind about recalling him, and it took a conciliatory performance by the Liverpool man to rescue his England spot, the loss of which he had felt so keenly.

Before that same match against Wales Revie had also dropped Kevin Keegan, who responded by storming out of the England hotel. As England had been about to depart for the previous match at Belfast, Keegan, who had once expressed sympathy with the position of Catholics in Ulster, had been the subject of a threatening telephone call received by Ted Croker at FA headquarters. Having elected to travel and play at possible personal risk, Keegan might have expected better reward than being left out for the next match. For Revie, who set so much store by public relations, Keegan's walk-out was a potential crisis, one he solved by contacting the Liverpool player and promising him a place in the next match against Scotland. It was curious *ad hoc* management, lacking the touch of a man who in the past had shown a much clearer idea of what he was doing.

Revie's dismissal of Alan Ball as captain showed a similar ham-fistedness. It came about in September 1975 as Ball was still in high feather after the splendid rout of Scotland. The first inkling of what was in store came not from Revie but from a journalist telephoning Ball to get some reaction at his being dropped. Then, in Ball's morning post and after the telephone call, the letter arrived. It contained no explanation and had not even been signed by Revie but instead by a secretary in his absence. For Ball, already confused and angry by the realisation that Fleet Street had been told some hours earlier, such a discourtesy was the final insult.

There would be no further words between Ball, veteran of 72 internationals, and Revie. As Ball groped around in his mind for some possible explanation, he was reminded of events at a three-day gathering of England players that Revie had organised at West Park Lodge. Ball had asked if the players might go out one evening, to which Revie had agreed on condition they returned by midnight. Few made it back before the early hours of the following day. Revie, Ball felt, held him responsible as captain, although he said nothing at the time. At Leeds, in Jimmy Lumsden's words, Ball might have been 'nailed'. But with England Revie seemed reluctant to face matters openly ; unable to put minor instances of player rebellion into perspective. Ball considered that Revie failed to understand how much playing for England mattered to him; that, as captain, he had no intention of challenging his manager's position.

Alan Hudson, another player who found the Revie regime uncomfortable to live with, was soon to be discarded. Yet Revie did not impose rules and regulations for their own sake; he was neither a bully nor a dictator. They were, Mike Channon feels, merely a symptom of Revie being wrapped up in the game. "He was so enthusiastic and he wanted everyone to have that same enthusiasm. I think he felt frustrated that everyone didn't feel the same as him. He liked everything right. I remember one day, the lads were messing about at West Park Lodge and Les Cocker got pushed into the pond. He got angry over that . . . that shouldn't happen to the training staff.

"In training, he went overboard with tactics. I don't think he needed to do that. Alf Ramsey simply said: 'This is what we're going to do . . . so and so take him.' We'd do a couple of little free kick routines and that would be the end of the story. Eventually with Revie, your mind was full of too much . . . you could end up a nervous wreck. Some would take the dossiers seriously, though to others they were a joke. Revie should have just said they were there if we needed them . . . and that's the way he meant them, to be fair to him. He was misunderstood. Players aren't really that intelligent. They didn't need all that. They just want to play football."

Now discarded, Ball was to start a campaign of guerrilla warfare against Revie through the press. But whatever shortcomings were attributed to the England manager, the teams he had picked, despite their various composition, had remained unbeaten through the nine international matches of his first year. Defeat was to arrive in October 1975, in a match of some importance, at Czechoslovakia in the European Championship. England lost 2-1. The encounter had had a false start the day earlier when play had begun in Bratislava before thick fog forced the match to be abandoned. It was not, Ted Croker considered, cause for undue alarm considering the Czechs had been at home and were an accomplished side. But three weeks later, England took part in a poor 1-1 draw against Portugal in Lisbon. Again, fundamental team changes were made, including the recall of Trevor Brooking whom Revie had discarded a year earlier. It was at this point that the dissenting voices started to become a chorus. Not only had England played badly, the point they had dropped meant almost certain elimination from the Championship finals.

In adversity, Revie's refrain was heard once more: that he must have more time with his players if England were to succeed. Again, he gained some ground. The FA and the League reached agreement whereby Revie could have players for nine days before a midweek international, providing they were released to play for their clubs on the intervening Saturday. But the concession was not obtained without a further attack on Revie from Alan Hardaker in which he declared that postponing matches would not have made a scrap of difference to events in Portugal. "We smacked of excuses before we left," Hardaker said. He followed up with a quite gratuitous swipe at Revie. "At present (with England), it is money, money, money."

Chapter Eleven

I N THE FACE of difficulties, Revie might have appreciated a *confidant* and the support of administrators at the FA. But while Ted Croker was a sympathetic listener, if not always in agreement with his ideas, the new FA chairman Sir Harold Thompson could scarcely have been less of a comfort to the England manager. Where his predecessor, Sir Andrew Stephen, had been kindly and considerate, Thompson was brusque and interfering. Many, including Croker, had troubled relations with the new chairman, but for Revie, Thompson reserved his worst manners. Merely regarding Revie with indifference seemed not to be enough. Thompson appeared more intent on humiliating him.

Sir Harold Thompson was an unlikely figurehead at the FA. His achievements had been in the field of chemistry of which he was Professor at Oxford University. While at Oxford, he had also been deeply involved in amateur football. Shortly after the war he had created Pegasus, a combined side of mature Oxford and Cambridge students which twice won the FA Amateur Cup. Thompson himself had played for his university. But it was, as Croker remarks drily, very far removed from the England team.

There was an early exchange between Revie and Thompson that later was to become celebrated. At a dinner, Thompson turned to the England manger and said: "When I get to know you better, Revie, I shall call you Don." Revie had a swift riposte. "And when I get to know you better, Thompson, I shall call you Sir Harold." It is one of Revie's few recorded flashes of wit.

Croker says: "Don obviously got the impression that Sir Harold didn't think too much of him. You could say that Thompson referring to Don as Revie might have been a typical schoolteacher thing but it wasn't, for he didn't call everybody by their surname. He chose to do that to Don and it was undoubtedly derisory. But it was public knowledge I didn't get on with Sir Harold either. He certainly was opinionated . . . he simply didn't have the capacity to get on with people. Yet the atmosphere between Don and other members of staff on the FA was generally less than ideal too. Everyone was aware of it."

Rudeness was one thing but interference in Revie's management was another. Thompson would think nothing of trying to meddle in team selection. "The classic one," Croker recalls, "was when Thompson told Don he shouldn't play Malcolm MacDonald after MacDonald had a particularly poor game. It puts a manager in a very difficult position. There is no way after that match that Revie would have played him. Yet he would think, 'If I don't play him, Thompson's going to think I'm listening to his advice.' " Afterwards, Croker reprimanded Thompson. "I said: 'Please don't ever make comments to the England manager about selection because it's just not fair.' Things were critical at the time."

Croker remains uneasy about further condemnation of Sir Harold Thompson. But Lord Harewood, a former president of the FA (though not while Thompson was its chairman), is less inhibited. "Towards Don, he behaved with incredible lack of tact and lack of knowledge," Lord Harewood says. "Thompson believed in getting his own way by order. He behaved stupidly with Don . . . he was a very arrogant man. And by then, Don, as a chosen England manager, was also not without a certain belief in his own powers . . . he certainly insisted on the last word in his area. Yet I think Thompson always wanted the last word.

He would talk openly against Don for quite a long time – he talked quite without any loyalty at all – with keenness to see Don pulled down. His interest in seeing Don exposed as an unsuccessful force was, in my view, greater than his interest in seeing England win. Don was very badly treated. I think he knew that and he didn't suffer it at all. I believe he had a much lower threshold of tolerance than one sometimes thought, and a quick sense of injustice."

Lord Harewood, with whom Revie still kept in quite regular contact, had a strong feeling of the England manager's frustration at not seeing his players week after week. "It wasn't really his team. It only became his team when they went into a big international competition. And I think he tended to over-prepare and that some of the people were bored by it."

The experiments continued. Revie's next match, against Wales to celebrate the centenary of the Welsh FA included such new caps as Peter Taylor, then playing in the Third Division with Crystal Palace, and Phil Boyer – players who had caught Revie's eye with their League performances but who were not of true international calibre. There followed the Home International Championships, won the previous year with a dynamic performance against Scotland, but 1976 was to be the year of the Scots' revenge. They beat England 2-1 at Hampden Park. Revie and England then decamped to America for the US Bicentennial Tournament in an effort to develop some cohesion before an important World Cup qualifier against Finland in Helsinki. They lost 1-0 to Brazil then beat Italy 3-2 in New York before concluding with a 3-0 victory over a Team America, a side drawn from the North American Soccer League. For the latter two matches Revie experimented once more, installing as captain Mike Channon, his most constant player.

Revie's 4-1 victory over the Finns gave grounds for some new optimism. At last, he seemed to have found a settled forward line in the shape of Stuart Pearson, Kevin Keegan and Channon. A midfield of Trevors – Francis, Cherry and Brooking – also looked as if it might be ripe for an extended run but was to be disrupted by injury. On 8 September 1976, for the friendly match against the Republic of Ireland at Wembley, the injured Channon was replaced by Charlie George for his one international appearance, and Ray Wilkins took Trevor Francis's place. The fumbling 1-1 draw, and the tentative 2-1 victory at Wembley over Finland in the second of their World Cup encounters, revived the old doubts. In a qualifying group where goal difference could be crucial there was an uneasy feeling of an opportunity having been lost.

Two months after the Republic of Ireland match, in November 1976, came Revie's sternest test. The Italians, playing for World Cup points in Rome, were likely to be much more fearsome than in the summer when playing in America. Again, Revie's team selections were various. This was the match for which he recalled Emlyn Hughes. He also recalled Stan Bowles of Queen's Park Rangers, having been swayed, as so often before, by Bowles's excellent club form. Revie's midfield selection, against a durable side renowned for its strength in defence, puzzled many. In choosing Trevor Cherry and Brian Greenhoff, both essentially defenders, he left England with little hope of having the craft to prise open the Italians. Neither had they; throughout the entire match they barely threatened the Italian goal. England were beaten 2-0.

There was little in the field of public relations that Revie could now do to deflect the abuse coming his way. Mike Channon, who believes he survived most of Revie's matches because there was no apparent replacement, recalls: "He couldn't believe the headlines he was getting. He was trying to do everything right but he was just having the mickey taken out of him. Like with the bingo, for instance. You sensed his frustration. He would always worry on tour that you would go out and have a few too many drinks and about the flak that could come back. One weekend we went to a health centre near Hungerford, and on the Saturday he told us to go off and have a day racing at Newbury. We did it and it hit the headlines. Suddenly, everything was news.

"Revie was a very nervous man . . . you could see that in him. He would sweat through nerves. I don't think he could trust anyone . . . he thought everybody was going to do him. That was my number one impression. I feel sorry for someone who can't trust anyone. It was just his manner . . . I always felt he double-checked. With his curfews, someone would come knocking at the door, say, to see if you wanted a sleeping tablet.

"As far as the team goes, I honestly don't think he ever picked the team he wanted. It was what the press said. For instance, he picked Stan Bowles to play in Italy for what was probably the biggest game of his managerial career. I thought Bowles played better in Italy than anyone. But for Revie, picking him was against the grain. It wasn't Don Revie. He seemed to be doing things he wasn't sure about. He was gambling though he didn't know when he was gambling, doing what the press wanted and hoping it would come right. It got to a stage when people were saying that you'd soon be able to buy England caps from Woolworths. They were being dished out far too readily. If you analyse it, you have to say he lost control. He was hoping and praying things would come right."

While some of the changes showed a dithering state of mind, Revie had also had the ill-luck to lose, through injury, his captain, Gerry Francis, centre-half Roy MacFarland and Colin Bell, who did not kick a ball in the 1976-77 season; a player Malcolm Allison once described as the best, most powerful runner in the business.

Qualification for the World Cup finals in Argentina was not yet beyond Revie but the chances were now arithmetical. While Luxembourg might be easy meat, they would also be easy meat for Italy. The Italian defeat was to be the beginning of the end. Yet still players noted that Revie's enthusiasm for the game remained undiminished, his thoroughness unabated. But his next opponents, three months later, were the Dutch at Wembley, a side of manifold talents. If the Italians had merely made suggestion of England's frailties, the Dutch, with Jan Peters and Johan Cruyff in indomitable form, declaimed them from the hilltops. Once more Revie had entered battle with unsuitable troops in midfield. Whatever the qualities of Paul Madeley and Brian Greenhoff, they could not shoulder the burden of trying to create England's attacking opportunities against a team of the calibre of Holland. Revie had also chosen Trevor Francis for this match.

By half time, England had been pulled to pieces and Revie was in a desperate state. "You're at Wembley, the home of football, and you've got your pride to play for," he told them. But there was nothing they could do. A defeat more shattering than the 2-0 scoreline suggested saw remaining reserves of confidence seep away and left Revie wondering where he might turn.

Against the feebler opposition, Italy had been making steady progress. They had won 4-1 against Luxembourg and 3-0 against

Finland. Revie's side would be required to score heavily in its two games against Luxembourg and beat the Italians at Wembley. In March, with seven more changes, England took a step on the way by beating Luxembourg 5-0. The arithmetic still insisted that the finals were not yet beyond England. But Revie felt under pressure and now he had soaking in his mind a lucrative approach to manage the United Arab Emirates national team; an opportunity that might give him security for life and deliverance from all the abuse he was suffering.

If the result against Luxembourg had provided him with some respite, the Home International Championships in May showed a team badly off form once more. Revie made no fewer than nine changes for the first game against Northern Ireland at Windsor Park in which England scraped a 2-1 victory with a goal three minutes from time. But it only set them up for two successive defeats. Wales, by winning 1-0, recorded their first ever victory at Wembley; and it left England ill-equipped to face Scotland whose raucous, marauding supporters celebrated their 2-1 victory by invading the pitch and digging up the goal-posts.

While Ted Croker admits there were some in the FA hostile to Revie, he rejects any notion that a conspiracy was underway to have him sacked. "There was never any talk at levels that mattered about a change of manager while the World Cup qualifying possibility was in existence," he says. On the other hand, Lord Harewood believes that Revie's fear for his future was justified. "I think inquiry was made by the FA of one club as to whether their manager might be let go [for England] under certain circumstances," he says.

A month after the Home Internationals, England embarked on a tour of South America. The Sunday before the start of the trip, the players were called together by Les Cocker and told he would be in charge for the early stages of the trip; that because of the flak Revie had been receiving, he would be resting for a few days. Several players suspected things were not as they should be, among them Mike Channon who says: "I thought there was something going wrong. He turned up in Buenos Aires but not in Brazil until the game. That wasn't like him."

They were also told by Cocker that Revie had flown out to Helsinki to watch the Italians in their World Cup qualifier against Finland. What no-one had discovered was that Revie had first flown to Dubai to clinch his deal with the United Arab Emirates at a time when Ted Croker, among others, assumed he was watching the Italians in training.

Revie arrived belatedly in South America looking, first of all, to be paid off. In Buenos Aires, he approached Dick Wragg, chairman of the FA International Committee. In that meeting, Revie told Wragg he was convinced he was about to be sacked. In the interests of minimum fuss, Revie proposed that his and Les Cocker's contracts should be paid up for the two remaining years, an exercise that would have landed the FA with a bill of £100,000. Wragg was astounded and told Revie there was no suggestion he was about to be sacked. Ted Croker, after hearing Revie's extravagant request, hurried to seek him out and told him he should see the job through.

"If he had come to me in the first place," Croker says, "I think he knew the response he would get. To say that he was throwing it in and leaving England in the lurch, and that he wanted paying off for the privilege was laughable. The whole idea was ludicrous. He was leaving the ship . . . we were in stormy waters . . . and he was asking for compensation at the same time. It just didn't make sense."

The tour continued. In playing terms, it had been more of a success than might have been expected and there was no sign that Revie's appetite for the game had dulled. England had drawn in Brazil, in Argentina and in Uruguay. Croker and his colleagues assumed they had heard the last of Revie's plans for a new life at the FA's expense; indeed, at the FA's summer conference two weeks after his meeting with Wragg, some members of the International Committee asked if he would consider renewing his contract. Revie mulled it over. Just over a fortnight later, the FA had its answer thrust in front of them on the front page of the *Daily Mail*. Revie would take no more of his thankless task.

The article appeared on 12 July 1977, just as Revie had turned 50. It conveyed the flavour of near despair; the outpourings of a man who felt ill-used and pilloried. "The past three years have been very rough for me and my family . . . the job was bringing too much heartache to those nearest to us. It was rough on my son and daughter and it's not very nice to hear your father constantly attacked. Nearly everyone in the country seems to want me out. So I'm giving them what they want," he told Jeff Powell. Two days later, the world discovered the price. Revie had signed a £340,000 four-year contract to manage the United Arab Emirates national side. There was a trace of bitterness about Revie's self-justification. "For years, everyone seems to have believed I've just been feathering my nest. So perhaps the time has come to put myself first for once," he said.

He catalogued the lucrative deals he had made on England's behalf and the profitable alternative jobs he had turned down in order to stay at Leeds United where, he claimed, he had constantly struggled to get a decent reward for his efforts. By now he was something of a battleground; still popular with his supporters but castigated by many who felt he had been greedy and deceitful. Two months later, the *Daily Mirror*, in search of its own scoop to counter the *Daily Mail*, was to embark on its saga of Revie's alleged attempts to fix critical matches while managing Leeds.

For Jeff Powell of the *Daily Mail* the scoop of his lifetime had begun with a telephone call from Revie, while in Leeds, suggesting that the two of them travel up to Scotland for the British Open Golf Championship. As Powell called in on Revie's home in Leeds, the England manager told him of his offer and of his conviction that Sir Harold Thompson was plotting to replace him. While the tone of the story might have been heavy with a sense of Revie being at the end of his tether, Revie was, Powell says, perfectly calm and sensible. Powell made his own way up to Scotland, telling his newsdesk that he had a hot story and would need cash to be made available to him for unlimited travel.

"When I came back, Don was ready to go. We set off together anonymously (Revie had assumed the name of his son Duncan) flying out via Switzerland and Athens for Dubai. Don was not (as was widely reported) in disguise. That would have been difficult though he did wear a flat cap. Meanwhile I had left behind two envelopes that included Don's letter of resignation to the FA."

Powell had also left two sealed envelopes at the *Daily Mail*. The first was opened the evening they reached Switzerland and contained the "Revie quits" story. The second, to be opened later, would have details of the England manager's new life in the Emirates. The letters, hand-delivered to the FA, reached Lancaster Gate between six o'clock and seven o'clock, after the headquarters were shut. Meanwhile, in Athens, the conspirators were spotted by a sharp-eyed Briton with a nose for a story "He happened to be a *Daily Mail* reader and it was our office he rang," Powell says. It proved a lucky escape for his scoop.

Powell says that Revie was not paid any money specifically for the story save to cover his "running expenses" such as air fares and travel, though two years later, when the ramifications of Revie's escapade took him to the High Court, the former England manager said in evidence that he was paid a "substantial sum." Rumours about the precise amount varied from £15,000 to £20,000. As Les Cocker was also taking flight with his boss, he too had to be accommodated, and was put up in a five star country house hotel so he could be out of circulation.

Even at the time Revie was, Powell recalls, concerned about the public image that he might acquire. The England manager was to find few who would defend the method of his departure, particularly because the *Daily Mail* story had appeared before his letter of resignation had reached officials at FA headquarters. His most abrasive critic, Bob Stokoe, says simply: "He should have been castrated for the way he left England."

Ted Croker feels the episode clinched Revie's reputation for money grabbing. For whatever purpose, he had received money from the *Daily Mail*. Croker had been conscious before of Revie's keenness to make money – through payment for interviews and after dinner speaking – yet he did not hold it against him. "It wasn't something I deplored in any way. I never knew him do anything dishonest. The fact that newspapers and television want to pay for certain facilities is, I think, fair game. The reason I think he was a bad England manager had nothing whatever to do with financial deals."

Lord Harewood describes Revie's behaviour at the time as tactless rather than wicked. "Telling the *Daily Mail* before the FA was a tremendous tactical mistake. It put him in the wrong though not as much, in my view, as the FA wronged him. I think he was incensed and wanted to secure his position. I don't think the way Don left was any worse than Sir Harold Thompson having been disloyal and plotting against him."

Bob English, former physiotherapist at Leeds United, had every sympathy for Revie. "I was brought up in a little country cottage in Ireland and if I'd been in his shoes, I would have grabbed twice as much . . . because, like me, he didn't have very much when he was young. He wanted to make sure his children and his family were looked after. I don't think he was greedy."

Johnny Giles, in the light of Revie's public self-reproach, says: "It's obvious he shouldn't have done it the way he did. He didn't do himself justice. He left himself open to savage criticism by telling the *Daily Mail* first. There was no defence for it. He ruined a lot of good work and then became a baddy . . . which he wasn't. But who isn't greedy? The people who write the stories in the tabloid newspapers might be the greediest in the world."

As time unfurled in Dubai, Revie's fears for his public image were justified. The *Mirror* stories containing the bribery allegations were in full swing. Though he had initiated legal proceedings, he would never, ultimately, sue. Powell, who made a couple of return trips to Dubai to see Revie, believes the possible costs deterred him from the courts. "In the end, I think he thought it wasn't going to be worth it," Powell says.

Revie would have litigation enough anyway. The FA was to take fierce retribution. The mood was, Ted Croker recalls, that Revie could not be allowed to get away with this breach of contract. Four days after the story appeared, the FA issued a statement revealing that it intended taking legal advice. (The FA had also to consider the matters unearthed in the *Daily Mirror* bribes stories but decided these were outside the scope of its inquiries as there was the likelihood of a civil court action.) An emergency committee comprising among others Revie's old enemy Sir Harold Thompson decided there was a case for Revie to answer and on 28 July the England manager was charged with bringing the game into disrepute.

The case was to be heard on 31 August. Four charges were laid against Revie; that by breaching his contract he had set a bad example to all; that by failing to tell FA officials of his dealings with Dubai when he had asked for his contract to be paid up, he had acted deceitfully; that by his alleged attempt to conceal his Dubai visit, he had debased his official position in English football; and that by telling the *Daily Mail* before the FA, he had breached his contract. Moreover, so the FA said, Revie had abandoned his post at a crucial time in the FA's international programme - there was still a theoretical possibility England could qualify for the World Cup finals. All this had damaged the image of football and the FA.

Revie's solicitors replied saying they did not accept the FA had any jurisdiction over him and that they would not attend the hearing. In the event, the commission sat on 17 September. Sir Harold Thompson insisted on presiding over it, much to Ted Croker's disquiet. Croker had advised him that as Chairman of the FA, the complaining party, Thompson could not be seen to be impartial. Croker was convinced it would have been possible to make alternative arrangements and find wise and knowledgeable neutrals.

The commission ruled that Revie be suspended from any involvement in football under the jurisdiction of the FA until he appeared before them and the matter be resolved. A year later, Revie responded, saying he would answer the charges. The hearing was to be 18 December 1978, the same day as Alan Ball appeared on charges of accepting irregular payments from Revie – the £300 with which the former Leeds manager was said to have tried to lure Ball from Blackpool to Elland Road. Ball was fined £3,000 after admitting two charges of accepting inducements but as the allegations were part of Revie's pending libel action against the *Daily Mirror*, the FA Commission, after protracted deliberations, decided to leave the matter alone.

Mr Gilbert Gray QC, appearing for Revie, claimed the FA had no jurisdiction over him and also that Sir Harold Thompson was unfit to sit in judgement as there was a real likelihood he would be biased against Revie. Among his evidence was a cutting from one national newspaper in which Thompson had been quoted as saying: "The recent events have been quite disgraceful . . . Revie has behaved very badly." Mr Gray said: "If this were a criminal court and a presiding judge had been quoted in the press as expressing such views . . . that judge would be debarred from sitting because it would be repugnant to natural justice." Both objections were over-ruled and the case proceeded, with Thompson both giving evidence and asking Revie questions; this after his rather preposterous declaration that he had an open mind.

Mr Gray told the hearing that the whole tradition of English football was about coming and going and that the man who isn't successful must either get out or fade out. Revie said that because his predecessor, Sir Alf Ramsey, had been asked to leave after a run of poor results, he felt it was only a matter of time before the same happened to him.

The history of Revie's tenure as England manager was turned over during the hearings. Curiosities were exposed, among them Revie's grievance that he had been expected to travel second class, instead of first class as stipulated by his contract. He had been frustrated by the slowness of decision-making: a commercial deal with Austin Reed had fallen through because the FA had taken six months to make up its mind. But above all, the pressures on himself and his family had been acute. The decision to accept the United Arab Emirates fortune was to secure his family's future, Revie told the commission. It did little to move the heart of his chief inquisitor. "The press and everyone else pillory me . . . it has an effect on my wife, children and everyone else . . . and I don't get paid. I don't think that argument is a terribly impressive one," Sir Harold Thompson said.

Revie told the commission that because of the efforts he had made to drum up interest in England, and the money he had brought in through commercial deals, he had been entitled to ask for the final two years of his contract to be paid up. At that time, he had not signed up for the United Arab Emirates. Mr Gray said : "We are dealing with ordinary professional footballers, managers and the rest, and to expect a meticulously high standard that might be more appropriate to the House of Convocation in Canterbury or York in this scenario is, in my submission, too extravagant by far."

While conceding Revie's departure may have lacked charm and frankness Mr Gray asked the commission to believe that he had always been very much a family man and it was his family he was thinking of; a matter not for criticism but for commendation. The commission responded by ordering Revie to be banned from involvement in English football for ten years from the date of his departure to the United Arab Emirates; a penalty so severe that it was bound to invite application by Revie's solicitors to the High Court for it to be overturned.

Obtaining justice as he saw it was to cost Revie dear. A re-enactment of his latter career, warts and all, would be played out in the High Court before Mr Justice Cantley in November and December 1979. Here, in the interests of having quashed the restraint of trade imposed on him by the FA commission, he was required to bare his soul during a hearing spread over 18 days.

On day two, there were graphic descriptions of his torment as England's results went against him: stories of insomnia, abusive fans throwing things at him and further details of his impossible relationship with Sir Harold Thompson, who had complained about the cost of an eight-day summer get-together of England players. Revie faced up to his own mistakes; the surfeit of team changes he had made and the irreverence with which some England players had treated his celebrated dossiers. "I found out later they were using them to keep the scores when they played cards at the hotel," he told the court.

During the 1977 England tour of South America, Revie said he had been so affected with nerves that he had lost his voice. He felt he could not have contributed a great deal to England's performances because the tension he was suffering would have been transmitted to the players. While managing England he had already rejected two alternative jobs, with Saudi Arabia and Barcelona. "I always felt the security of my position with England was very precarious . . . I think in football, the word is fear – fear of losing one's job and not being able to find another." Even at the peak of his career, Revie seemed forever haunted by a sense of insecurity and fear of the dole queue that his father had had to endure.

Conscious of the reputation for greed he had now acquired, Revie denied having ever asked for £5,000 tax free from the FA in addition to his request that his and Les Cocker's contracts should be paid up. Mr Justice Cantley, whose palpable distaste for Revie became one of the celebrated features of the proceedings, made public his disbelief. Agreeing with an FA member who said Revie acted deceitfully, the judge was to add at the end: "It was also, of course, greedy."

When Sir Harold Thompson came to give evidence, he would recall only two instances of alleged friction between him and the England manager: over Revie's desire to pull out of a game in Belfast against Northern Ireland on account of the troubles, and because he felt too much money was being spent on the England team. He denied in one breath ever having attempted to interfere with Revie's team selections, while saying in another: "I can't see why the chairman of the FA can't express his opinion on the performance of players."

Thompson said the magnitude of public reaction to Revie's resignation was enormous – "as much as if there had been an outbreak of war" – and that the extent of the general indignation was caused by the enormous amount being paid to Revie: not only £240,000 for a four-year contract but an additional £100,000 signing-on fee. Asked to comment on his statement that Revie had behaved badly, Thompson said: "I believe that to be true, so did my colleagues in the FA and, so far as one could tell, so did nearly everyone in the country."

Yet Revie was not wholly without support during the hearing. Lord Harewood spoke up for him and he was also backed by, among others, Johnny Giles, the television soccer pundits Jimmy Hill and David Coleman, and fellow soccer managers Jock Stein and Lawrie McMenemy, all appearing as character witnesses. There was also, according to Elsie Revie, the warmth and support of many people in the street. "We took taxis between our hotel and the court every day of the hearing. Not one driver would take the fare and every one of them wished us luck," she told one journalist. But Mr Justice Cantley had clearly decided he would not be susceptible to testimonies in favour of Revie. It must have been with almost agonised reluctance he decided that, whatever he thought of the former England manager, Revie should win back his right to work in English football.

The case had been decided on the likelihood of bias by Sir Harold Thompson and his fellows on the FA commission. Mr Justice Cantley, as Ted Croker had feared all along, ruled that the remarks he had made to two national newspapers had cast doubt upon Thompson's impartiality – "however hard he tried to be fair, as I am sure he did" – though he dismissed almost all the instances of personal hostility alleged against the former England manager by Revie himself and Lord Harewood.

Then, having got out of the way the distasteful business of finding for Revie (though rejecting his claims that the FA had exceeded its powers by imposing a ten-year ban) the judge warmed to his mission of heaping as much personal abuse on Revie as his two-hour summing-up would allow. "Notorious . . . prickly . . . utterly selfish . . . lacking in candour . . . brooding on imagined wrongs." Most of the arguments alleging Sir Harold Thompson had been hostile to Revie were "scraping the barrel". Of Thompson himself, the judge concluded: "I am glad to be able to wholly acquit Sir Harold of bad faith. He is an honourable man who deplores the coarse comments, materialism and selfish greed which, from time to time, obtrude in professional football." But Revie had "presented to the public a sensational and notorious example of disloyalty, breach of duty, discourtesy and selfishness. His conduct brought English football, at a high level, into disrepute."

Neither protagonist was in court to savour Mr Justice Cantley's considered opinion. As Mr Gray submitted a claim for costs on Revie's behalf, he said: "It is apparent, if I may say so, that there may not be a great deal of warmth moving to Mr Revie from any direction." To which the judge retorted : "I haven't exhibited any more than I can help." Justice Cantley did not award Revie the damages he had sought and ordered him to pay two-thirds of his own costs. For the FA, which had to swallow the lion's share of the estimated £50,000 legal bill, it was, as Ted Croker said, an expensive and sorry episode. The FA had also lost its counter-claim for damages on grounds that Revie's departure "materially prejudiced" England's chances of qualifying for the World Cup Finals, and that by failing to qualify, they lost large profits.

Lord Harewood, at Revie's side for much of the hearing says: "I think it was an agony for him and the elements of character assassination on the part of the defending counsel grilling him were very unattractive. The summing-up of the judge was one of the craziest things I have ever read. I think that judge was extremely ill-versed in human behaviour . . . he was an ass. If he really thought that Sir Harold Thompson had behaved admirably and Don hadn't, then he is a very, very poor judge of character . . . and of evidence. He plainly disbelieved every word I said but I don't give a bugger what he thought."

Ted Croker, although representing the opposition, agrees. "I didn't like the way Cantley handled it at all. I thought his summing-up was very wrong, his assessment of the various characters totally wrong . . . he praised Sir Harold Thompson to the hilt as being an honourable man. I didn't think it was fair and he should not have worried so much about the personalities." Certainly, Croker was not for bearing a grudge against Revie after the proceedings. "We always had a very amicable relationship . . . no reason not to. Revie knew my views and admitted to me personally that he should never have done what he did."

Chapter Twelve

REMOTE FROM all he knew, Don Revie nevertheless looked to home, and to the past, to create a new beginning for football in the United Arab Emirates. His first recourse was to the stalwarts who had served him at Leeds so he took with him Les Cocker, and also approached Syd Owen, then still coaching at Birmingham City. "Don sent me a letter from the Emirates asking me to go out there to organise football within the schools there and try and develop the younger talent for the future of the professional team. But I'd served in the Middle East during the last war and I'd seen enough of sand. So, reluctantly, I turned it down," Owen says.

Revie's ordeal in the High Court took place more than two years after he arrived in the United Arab Emirates. There he found temperatures that reached 120 degrees Fahrenheit in high summer, and a drenching humidity; conditions that made football impossible in June, July or August. For the rest of the year, a much drier atmosphere and temperatures around 80 degrees enabled soccer to be played.

Revie found also that the playing facilities were in transition.

Some clubs still performed on sand pitches. But changes were on the way: 12 out of the 14 clubs in the Emirates first division had ordered artificial turf pitches; one ground was having a £7 million facelift and work had begun on a national stadium that would cost £25 million. If Revie's mission there were to founder, it would not be for the lack of resources.

On arrival, Revie declared that he had never believed he would be able to live abroad. "I've always known myself to be the typical Englishman," he said. It was not as if he were travelling within Western Europe, to another recognisable culture. But at least life in the Emirates was less austere than in other Islamic Arab states: there was no prohibition on having a cold beer or two.

Revie's thoroughness, belief in youth and appetite for the game remained undimmed, despite the vicissitudes of his latter England years. There was much for him to enjoy, not least a princely salary and a luxurious lifestyle. But things were not perfect. "I think he minded that Elsie didn't really take to it at all," says Lord Harewood. "There was nothing for her to do. He was to be with his team. I think she could play golf but there was no social life at all. He minded that there weren't people to make friends with and there was little for Elsie. Although he was only out there months at a time, it was for some years. I think he came back somewhat disillusioned by the whole thing but I don't know what disillusioned him. He never told me."

Revie was to have three years as national team coach, enjoying much greater control over players than he had while managing England. Constructing a workable playing system from scratch greatly appealed to his organisational abilities. He was dismissed from the post in May 1980, on the grounds that management decided it wanted an Arab-speaking coach. It was an amicable parting of the ways with Revie receiving substantial unspecified compensation and being given a farewell party and presentation. He was entitled to be satisfied with his efforts. "We lost only one of our last nine games at national level. I am leaving a squad of good young players and am very happy about the whole business," he said.

During his stay, Revie was, Lord Harewood recalls, surprised more than once by one or two of the local customs. In keeping with his managerial style, Revie would take players away before a match to help build up team spirit before the game. "It was also the idea that they should be away from their wives," Lord Harewood says. "But he started taking one of his teams away and they all seemed to be exhausted the next morning. What he hadn't twigged was that they were quite as happy to pop into each other's beds as they were into bed with their wives or girlfriends. Much more dangerous . . . much more experimental. Don was very naïve in some ways . . . he was not a man of the world in sexual relations. The idea of this had never crossed his mind. I think possibly he had a prudish side to his character."

Revie was not slow to find alternative employment. Soon he was hired to manage the UAE first division club Al Nasr, owned by Sheik Mana Bin Khalifa Almaktoum, and recruited as assistant Eric Smith, the wing-half signed by Leeds from Celtic in 1960, who had been first Revie's team-mate then his charge at Elland Road.

Smith recalls: "I contacted Don in 1980, after Les Cocker had gone home. I was at a club nearby, Sharjah, and Don had given me a good reference – before that, I was in my sixth year with Hamilton Academicals. At Al Nasr, Don created the youth programme and in the first year he was manager, they just missed the championship by goal difference in a league of 14."

The extent of the youth programme created by Revie and overseen by Smith is remarkable. Smith says: "I had eight coaches under me and in eight months we coached groups of boys in two-year age groups between eight and 18. One day the sheik wanted to know where all the money was going . . . on Coca Colas and sandwiches. I told him we had had 22,834 attendances at the coaching sessions in those eight months . . . Don had organised it and I supervised. That is what the man was about – he got the club on its feet.

"You spent ten months out of twelve in the UAE. The lifestyle was what Don deserved . . . like Hollywood, with a super house and swimming pool. Elsie and Don and me and my wife were like a family for those years. We had picnics and used the sheik's beach . . . he had a quarter of a mile of private sands. Duncan and Kim were always coming out. But Don must have spent £15,000 to £20,000 flying people out to see him. He loved the people he loved."

The Al Nasr side fashioned by Revie had several promising seasons challenging for honours. He was not to see all the fruit of the youth policy he engineered – four of the players he had nurtured played for the United Arab Emirates in the 1990 World Cup. But despite his efforts, Revie's employment at Al Nasr was ended quite arbitrarily. Smith recalls: "There was an announcement in the newspapers we were staying. I don't know what happened but a month later we had to leave. We didn't ask why. We had finished third in the league with a young team. You can ask the sheik but he won't give a reason. It was sheer rubbish for the work that had been done. The next year, they finished third from bottom. Don had created the basis of the national team and set things up. He was brilliant."

Revie could afford the time to look around for a new job. Since the High Court had lifted the FA ban that would have excluded him from English football for ten years, he was now drawing £10,000 a year from Leeds United, the fruits of the consultancy deal he had had the foresight to make before leaving for the England job in 1974. It was a role that had the potential of undermining any full-time Leeds manager. In practice, though, it did not. At the time, Eddie Gray had been appointed, assisted by Jimmy Lumsden. Lumsden recalls: "Don Revie came to a few games and would come into the dressing-room offering advice but not in the way as if he were trying to tell you your job. He would probe away and ask a couple of things and hope we would ask him things, which we did. He would give up the benefit of his experience. We held him in such high respect, we would just listen to every word."

It was almost as if the spirit of Revie had come alive again at Elland Road during that time. The club was, once again, having to find its feet in the Second Division but Gray and Lumsden were nurturing the best crop of young players seen at Elland Road for more than 20 years; Scott Sellars, John Sheridan, Andy Linighan, Denis Irwin. Revie predicted: "If everyone is patient and Eddie is left alone they will be knocking on the door for promotion, next season if not this." But the Leeds directors were not to allow Gray the time he needed and the chance for them to mature together. When he was sacked and Billy Bremner succeeded him, many were sold quite cheaply, establishing themselves elsewhere before realising their considerable playing and money potential.

Meanwhile in August 1984, Revie had headed east again, taking up a two-year contract to manage Al-Al FC in Cairo. But he stayed only a few months. His wife Elsie, who had endured the cultural strangeness of the United Arab Emirates for six years, had had enough. She was ill and unhappy. There was nothing for Revie to gain by staying. He was hardly desperate for the money. While he relished any football challenge, he decided another two years in Egypt was not worth the family sacrifice. By 1984, his exile from England was over.

His eagerness for football management, however, remained great. Aged 57, having run two national sides and three club sides in assorted corners of the world, Revie found himself chasing the managerial vacancy at Queen's Park Rangers as soon as he returned home. "I never thought I'd have the chance to get back into the English game but I have discovered I have missed the involvement. I've been away seven years and don't know everything about First Division players. But I'm still able to get on to the training pitch and after 40 years, I feel I have something to offer the game," he said.

It would have been one of the fascinating soccer experiments. But it was not to work out. Not for the first time, Revie's affairs stumbled over the question of money. According to Jim Gregory, the Queen's Park Rangers chairman, Revie increased his demands as he went along. Gregory had met Revie the day after a telephone conversation in which the appointment had been discussed. "The terms he asked for then were not those he was seeking when I met him," Gregory observed at the time. "In view of his increased demands, I have unfortunately come to the conclusion that I no longer wish Mr Revie to be the new manager of Queen's Park Rangers."

Revie was angry and disappointed. It was to be the last job in football he would seek either at home or abroad. Although he would never lose his love of the game, he had other things with which to fill his life. The Revies had a villa near Marbella by a golf course and, on their return to England, bought a house in Surrey next to the golf course at Wentworth. In golf, Revie had always found relaxation and escape. When managing Leeds, he would play with friends at Temple Newsam on Sundays, and there was one golden rule: that there was to be no mention at all of football.

Johnny Giles recalls seeing Revie after his return from the Middle East. "Probably for the first time in his life, he was relaxing. I think at that stage, he was feeling more secure than he had ever felt before." But Revie had not totally relinquished the world of work. His son Duncan, having gone from Repton to Cambridge where he graduated in law, had found the legal profession too stuffy for his liking and abandoned it for the business of marketing packaged trips to top sporting events. By this time, Duncan was running his own company, Total Sport, with Revie senior acting as part-time consultant. It was an arrangement that suited them both. Duncan found that despite the notoriety that had surrounded his father's departure from managing England, the Don Revie name still carried plenty of clout. "It's incredible how famous he is," Duncan told one journalist. "He's been out of football for ten years but he still stops the traffic."

The ambitions in education Revie had for Duncan had been fulfilled, although his son's departure from the conventional path of graduating to life in a solicitor's office had come as something of a shock. But Duncan's entrepreneurial new career gave Revie the chance to exercise once more his well-honed public relations skills. Of his father, Duncan said: "He's got a brilliant touch. That's why he was one of the greatest managers of all time." Meanwhile, his father was still expressing soccer ideas: his old desire to see the game played on Sundays during the summer, and a new theory that players should be trained at three in the afternoon rather than in the morning, so they would be better attuned to kick-off time. Revie's football soul was ever-enduring.

From Wentworth, the Revies moved once again, in 1986, this time to surroundings in which Elsie would feel at home. Their new home was in Kinross, Perthshire, not far from Lochgelly, the village in which she had been brought up. It was to be the final of Revie's happy and not so happy wanderings, a move made with contentment and relaxation most in mind but one that would instead be associated with his desperate and painful last years.

When, in the summer of 1986, Revie came home from playing a round of golf at St Andrews complaining that the backs of his legs ached, neither he nor Elsie thought too much about it. He was a bit out of practice and, at the age of 59, entitled to the odd twinge, though he could still go round a course in 79 shots. But suddenly and persistently, he was starting to get pains in the backs of his legs during the last half dozen or so holes of each round. It was a nuisance to him but at first it never occurred to Revie there might be anything sinister. It was, he thought, perhaps to do with a slipped disc problem he'd had going back years.

The next month, the Revies went golfing in Spain. There, Elsie noted the curious way Don was moving his left foot. Revie also complained of a strange sensation that left him feeling as if he were floating. He returned to England to consult his doctor in Leeds who ruled out the disc problem because no nerves were trapped. Meanwhile, Revie battled on playing golf but it was clear to everyone his health was deteriorating. When he fell and hurt his knee, alarm grew in the Revie family.

In February 1987 Don Revie played his last round of golf. Specialists began to carry out exhaustive tests as further problems manifested themselves. Revie realised he was starting to lose the use of his hands when he found himself fumbling to do up a button. In May, he was called to London to see a specialist. Filled with a sense of foreboding, Revie arranged for Duncan and Kim to accompany him. Together, they sustained the dreadful diagnosis. The consultant announced that Revie had motor neurone disease, that the nerves were not strong enough to keep the muscles going. There was no operation, no cure. The three Revies burst into tears on the spot.

For Don Revie, it was the cruellest thing imaginable. A man whose whole life had been based on sport and vigorous activity faced a painful and inexorable decline into crippledom and death. He was a classic victim. The disease, in which motor neurones in the brain die off and cause muscles gradually to waste away, is twice as frequent in men as in women and usually strikes people aged between fifty and sixty. Leg pains similar to cramp and weakness in the hands are the first symptoms. In its later stages, the victim has difficulty breathing, with contractions of the tongue eventually leading to loss of voice.

Throwing herself into a search which, against all the odds, might lead to somewhere her father could find respite, Kim Revie rapidly became a lay expert on the disease and where research into it was most advanced. Eventually she discovered a hospital in Houston, Texas, and in August 1987 the family flew out there clutching at the hope anyone would have had: that the diagnosis was wrong, that there was, after all, something that might alleviate the worst symptoms.

But instead, only the worst was confirmed. The Revies learned grim statistics: that 70 per cent of motor neurone disease victims die within three and five years of contracting the illness. Yet if Don Revie had been an American citizen, there was a three-year programme and a special experimental drug for which he would have been eligible. To know that, yet to be despatched back to England and denied the opportunity of such treatment, must only have added to the family's sense of despair.

Returning to his bungalow in Kinross, Revie gradually became accustomed to the new routine necessary for his shrinking life. He acquired a specially designed electrically operated chair that tipped him on to his feet, and large lightweight cutlery. Coordinating a shave with an electric razor would take him almost an hour. At a nearby hospital, he underwent a three-hour daily ritual of exercises. But gradually, he was losing control of all his limbs. As he became reduced to taking a five minute walk every few hours aided by a stick, Revie said: "I expect the left leg to follow the right up steps. But it doesn't – and I go down."

If nothing else, Revie was full of fighting talk. Nostalgic by nature, he looked back to his management days, in search of inspiration from the great battles Leeds United had had against overwhelming odds. The knowledge that he had a fatal disease had not, as he feared it might, sent him mad. "Fight it. Fight it all the way," he said. Revie had the moral support of many people besides his family, yet found he missed most of all the sort of geeing-up his greatest friend in football management, Bill Shankly, might have provided. The two had always shared a Saturday night telephone conversation even when the rivalry of Liverpool and Leeds was at its height. Shankly, Revie reckoned, would have told him not to believe the doctors and would have said instead: "You'll be fine."

When Revie's plight had become public, he and his family were inundated with letters. Some, in which the relatives of motor neurone sufferers described the agonies their loved ones had endured, made unbearable reading. Others, as far as was possible, cheered Revie up. Among the sympathetic correspondents was George Tinsley, the boy with whom Revie had grown up in Middlesbrough. Revie, even in the advanced stages of his illness, never abandoned his good habit of replying to correspondence. He was helped in this by his former secretary Jean Reid, who had been with him at Leeds and when he was manager of England. Tinsley has the letter still; a brief, nostalgic note that thanked him first of all for writing, then said: "I often look back, George. It was a good job you had that leather football, so I could practice with a real ball."

In May 1988, there would be another occasion for nostalgia. Many of the great players that Revie had reared at Elland Road came together once again to play a benefit match in his honour, the money being split between research into motor neurone disease and the Leeds Children in Need campaign. For many, that return visit to Elland Road was the first occasion in years that they had encountered their former boss, who was now confined to a wheelchair. "It was cruel for someone associated with the physical side of life," says Joe Jordan. Johnny Giles recalls: "He was bad . . . he couldn't move his arms . . . but he didn't want to talk about it." For Billy Bremner, it was a poignant occasion. "He was crying a bit that night and reminiscing about us. He loved reminiscing. I saw him in the early stages of his illness and he was reminiscing about his Manchester City days." Lord Harewood recalls: "It was very moving and Don was in good form although totally incapacitated and blown-up by steroids or whatever they were giving him. I spoke quite a lot to him although we were talking superficialities. Don didn't even stay for the game. He couldn't take the strain . . . there was too little resilience left."

It was public proof, if any were needed, that a lurid and sensational story published less than three months earlier in the *News Of the World*, claiming Revie had been cured, was a nonsense. It was, perhaps, the last occasion in his lifetime that Revie would be ill-used in the press. The *News of The World* story claimed Revie was on the way to a full recovery after 'revolutionary treatment' in a Moscow hospital paid for by his former employer at Al Nasr, Sheik Mana Bin Khalifa Almaktoum. Revie, so it was claimed, was walking again, having taken injections of a compound based on vitamins from grasses, weeds and herbs together with muscle-building steroids and interferon, the drug used in cancer treatment. Previously, the treatment had been tried only on rats and cats, so the story ran.

A deficiency in the article, based on alleged interviews with the sheik and a doctor said to have spent much time with Revie in search of a cure, was lack of confirmation by the Revie family. Possibly the only true line in it was that Revie had made a trip to Moscow. That much was confirmed by Foreign Office officials. The following day, a bleak little paragraph appeared in *The Independent*. It read: "Don Revie, the former Leeds United and England manager who is suffering from the incurable motor neurone disease, has not been miraculously cured as reported in the *News of the World*, his wife Else said." Behind those words must have lain unimaginable distress.

The previous year, when he could still get about with the aid of a stick, Revie had booked some suites in the clubhouse for the 1990 British Open Golf Championship due to be held at St Andrew's. It was a show of defiant optimism. He was not to make it. The illness which more than once Revie had likened to Leeds United playing Liverpool at Anfield, where the odds were always stacked against his team, overcame him on 26 May 1989. Revie died in Murrayfield Private Hospital in Edinburgh. He had suffered a vicious disease, its cause still unknown, although doctors in America had suggested that diet and stress could be at the root of it. Revie had endured enough stress for a hundred lives and, however fit he may have been, the number of years in which he had lived on his nerves would not have enhanced his health.

When the news broke, the gates of Elland Road were soon bedecked with scarves and posters in tribute to the man who had given Leeds United all the success it had ever known. Four days after his death, Revie's funeral took place at the Warriston Crematorium in Edinburgh, an occasion which reunited not only former Leeds players but other admirers, among them Lawrie McMenemy, whose managerial career Revie had encouraged, and Kevin Keegan. A bottle of cognac, Revie's favourite drink, adorned the lid of his coffin; a cheerful memento of the seemingly rare occasions he had been able to relax and enjoy life's small, uncomplicated pleasures.

Chapter Thirteen

A T HIS DEATH, few spoke ill of Revie. His former Leeds players lined up to pay tribute to him. While the words may have differed, the sentiments were consistent: that he was the best football manager there had ever been and that also he had given them training for life. Eddie Gray: "He wasn't just a manager to me. I went to Leeds United as a 15-year-old and more or less grew up with him. He brought me along in life and was more like a father than a manager." Trevor Cherry: "He treated me like a son. I owe a great deal of what I've got now and what I have achieved to Don." Jack Charlton: "Don made Leeds into one of the best teams this country has seen and certainly the best family club I have known. No-one wanted to leave Elland Road and that says everything."

The *Daily Mirror* in its reports of Revie's death was still snapping at its alleged bribes scandal. Like a dog worrying a tired bone, the paper had, two years earlier, demanded to know of Ted Croker why the FA had never fully investigated its allegations since Revie dropped his libel action. The rest of the newspaper world save *Today*, which saw fit to make no mention at all of Revie's death, was more magnanimous. In writing his obituaries, the press that had so tormented Revie in life gave his achievements balanced, even favourable, consideration. Jeff Powell wrote: "A friend of mine died yesterday . . . a big loveable bear of a man . . . released at last from the controversy which clouded the summit of his career." In *The Times*, David Miller wrote that Revie "was distinguished throughout more than 30 years as a player and a manager by the intelligent thought which he attempted to bring to football . . . as a journalist, I found him to be one of the most honest managers I ever dealt with."

These are not the reflections of naïve men, yet they are at odds with views of others in the same trade, who viewed Revie's apparent honesty with cynicism; that it was merely slick public relations. "At the time he left England, I would say he was crucified by the press. But I think that was because some journalists felt let down that I had got the story and they hadn't," Powell says.

Some of that may be true. The circumstances of Revie's departure gave newspapers ill-disposed towards the former England manager a stick with which to beat him. It was clear from the ferocity of the attacks that some held Revie's entire career in little or no esteem. Yet the singular thing about Revie is the extreme and opposite reaction his name provokes in almost every sphere of football; administration, refereeing, management, playing, as well as sports writing. It is not just a question of emphasis. He was loved and hated, admired and despised, trusted and distrusted all at the same time.

Bob Stokoe, the memory of an alleged bribery attempt by Revie still vibrant in his mind after almost 30 years, says: "It has always riled me when I see the career Revie has had. At the back of my mind, the bribe is always there. He was always an evil man to me." Less emotionally, Revie's management has also been castigated by Bill Nicholson, the former Tottenham manager, principally for the on-field gamesmanship employed by his players. Yet Len Shackleton, a Revie critic, pays him this double-edged compliment: "I would love to have played for him. He was a sufficient bastard . . . in the kindest sense . . . a great-motivator." Meanwhile Billy Bingham, another of Revie's managerial contemporaries, is so protective of his memory that he declined to be interviewed for a book that did not have the official blessing of the Revie family.

Among referees, opinion is similarly diverse. Clive Thomas has said that with its relentless harassment and contesting of decisions on the field, Don Revie's Leeds United gave him more trouble than the other First Division clubs put together. Yet Jack Taylor says: "Revie was personally charming. I have all the time in the world for him. He was never anything other than honest and frank." Revie researched referees as diligently as he investigated every other aspect of the game. Of Taylor, he rarely had cause for complaint; it would not have been with Taylor in mind that Revie once made a clumsy approach to Alan Hardaker requesting that a more favourable referee be put in charge of one of Leeds United's games.

Had the referee in question been Ray Tinkler, it would have been no surprise. Of all Revie's mishaps with referees, those involving Tinkler probably caused him the most grief. Revie's furtive approach to Tinkler in 1965 in which he asked the official not to record a caution against Billy Bremner was an embarrassing folly, as vivid an illustration as any of his obsession with fixing whatever he could, however he could, in Leeds United's favour. Six years later, Tinkler's notorious offside decision that almost certainly cost Leeds a critical league match against West Bromwich, provoked from Revie a rare tirade and further censure. Tinkler has declined to give his own perspective on those difficult encounters with Revie. Jack Taylor recalls: "He was due to referee a Leeds game about a fortnight afterwards but that was changed." That decision may have been taken not with the aim of mollifying Revie but of ensuring Tinkler's personal safety.

How far would Revie go to win?. His dossiers, the pressures his team applied on referees, his attempted machinations with officials and administrators seem like the work of a desperado. The *Daily Mirror* bribes scandal, a murky affair that is still reluctant to yield all its secrets, contaminated the latter stages of his career. Of those approached, Bob Stokoe tells the most unswerving tale, a tale he has told a hundred times yet not one he ever marketed, for it was the *Mirror* that approached him.

The whole bribes saga began not in 1977 but in 1972 when the *Sunday People* became interested in events surrounding the previous season's match at Wolverhampton. A team from the Mirror was about to investigate a different and less sensational scandal, of turnstile fiddles at football grounds, when it stumbled across the *People*'s inconclusive story and saw in it more potent possibilities. It became an epic investigation involving 50 reporters, some travelling abroad to winkle out witnesses and evidence. Yet there is a creaking unease about the final product, sometimes a sense of words having been put into mouths, or else of inhibiting lawyers at the shoulders of the witnesses.

Although the series of *Mirror* stories did not appear until the September, Revie had become aware of the newspaper's investigations three months earlier. When he learned of Gary Sprake's involvement, Revie sought a meeting at a Leicester hotel but arrived to learn he had been stood up. Sprake had signed a contract with the *Mirror*. He told a story alleging Revie had used intermediaries to approach Jim Barron, the Nottingham Forest goalkeeper, to help throw away a League game Leeds had to win by a big score as they chased the League and Cup double in 1971-72.

Sprake now regrets the episode and his version of events further confuses the matter. He says: "I never made allegations that Revie tried to bribe people or get them to throw games. It was very unfortunate." Yet it is in keeping with statements made by Mike O'Grady and Stan Anderson 13 years later: that they too never made the somewhat tentative allegations attributed to them.

In the High Court, Sir Harold Thompson was of the opinion that allegations that Revie had tried to fix matches while in charge of Leeds were "a remarkable story which it would be very difficult to fabricate without an enormous imagination." Even in the context of a ruthless circulation war among tabloid newspapers, to have published a series of such defamatory stories in bad faith would have been to gamble on Revie's lack of stomach, or funding, for a libel battle. And had Revie been as wholly innocent as he protested, would not such a slur have been a case for defending his honour at all costs?

Yet to believe the stories opens up almost fantastic possibilities: a vision of Revie trekking off to football matches, his pockets full of ready cash with which to lead opposing players into temptation. Where might he have obtained such money and by whose authority? Lord Harewood considers several of the *Mirror's* witnesses were "tainted", and looking for financial help. Peter and Margaret Veitch doubt Revie had it in him to try and fix matches. Peter Veitch says: "From what we knew, he was basically a very simple and honest person. It would have brought his team into disrepute; his family into disrepute. The implications would have been unbelievable."

The whole affair may crave that verdict unique to Scottish justice: Not Proven.

What Revie did for Leeds United is not open to question. He created a team the memory of which will survive indefinitely. Years after he had left Elland Road and times were hard once again, there was a swagger about the supporters, a feeling that Leeds United had a right to glory; a demand that the club must, at all costs, regain its position among the élite. Before the Revie era, such feelings had never existed among Leeds United supporters, as Johnny Giles points out. "Leeds wasn't a big football area," he says. "The Leeds support of today is a legacy of what Don did. He wanted it to be a football area but that takes time. Who from those days would believe today the crowds that follow Leeds?

"It all happened too quickly at Leeds. They failed to appreciate it. They only do so since they struggled to get back into the First Division . . . they're nutters now. After we reached the Cup final in 1965, things never stopped. The support did build up; we were averaging nearly 40,000 in the last season. And what you see today is the legacy; they went mad to have it back.

Whatever Don did at Leeds cannot be taken away. The basic fact is that he took over a team in a down and out area with no players and turned it into one of the greatest teams the world has ever seen. It was a hard-working club with good characters and, structurally, the side changed very little. Don Revie did one of the great jobs in football by going to a non-footballing area and creating that team from nothing. All the other great managers came from footballing areas: Shankly, Busby, Nicholson. Leeds was a Rugby League area."

The ascendancy of Rugby League over soccer in Leeds before the Revie era is also spoken of by Norman Hunter, even if he exaggerates the drawing power of the former. Hunter will have no criticism of Revie, not even for the way he abandoned England. "I think there were a lot of things going on behind the scenes . . . that is an area I wouldn't comment on. Whatever he did as far as I was concerned was right. When I was sacked from one of my clubs I went to Marbella and we played golf together. That was basically the closest I've ever been to him. Yet the relationship was still one of teacher and pupil. That will never, ever change."

It is a remarkable expression of loyalty from one of Revie's favourite players, yet not uncommon among his football family. Even Revie's pre-match parlour games, so derided by some of the wayward spirits who played for England, are not to be mocked among the ranks of his great Leeds team. Hunter says: "There were grown men there that thoroughly enjoyed their bingo, their carpet bowls. We would run a book. It was all taken very seriously." Peter Lorimer recalls: "Everything we did was competitive. I've still got it in me now, even if I play a little game with the kids."

The superstitious side of Revie's nature that sometimes infected his Leeds team with uncertainty was, Johnny Giles feels, inextricable from the other aspects of his character that together made him such an effective manager. "It was because of some of those superstitions that Don was driven, and made Leeds United what they were. Don, like anyone else, wasn't perfect. But if he hadn't tried to be the perfect manager and hadn't the things about him that people later on said were his faults, Leeds United would not have done what they did."

Superstition and an apparent lust for money in his later years may all have been aspects of a sense of insecurity which many who knew Revie saw in him. In 1962, when Revie was still a relatively young man and struggling to get to grips with managing Leeds, his father had died. It was perhaps unsurprising he would put so much effort into creating his own families, and looked towards the confident self-made millionaire Harry Reynolds as a father figure. Years later, Peter Veitch recalls being at a party in Harrogate with Revie. "I was about the same size as Don, the same age, and this lady came up to him and asked him of me: 'Is this your brother?' And he said: 'I wish it was' . . . not because he had anything for me personally but because I think he would have liked a family."

In Revie's latter years as manager, he moved into Three Chimneys, a large luxurious house in north Leeds with an annexe, bought for the club by its chairman Manny Cussins then let to Revie at a peppercorn rent. (Later Revie acquired it, sold it and moved to a bungalow nearby.) In such surroundings, Revie could give expression to his desire for a family life: Elsie's mother, then two uncles and aunts came to live with them. "With Don, the family thing also extended to the players' wives," Peter Veitch says. "In the early years they were mostly single fellows and in some cases he vetted the kind of girls the lads went out with. But he didn't allow the lads to be exploited. When Leeds won the League Championship, the boss of the company I worked for put a do on for them at Harrogate. He said it would be nice if a player and his wife could sit at each table. Don didn't want that. All the players had to sit together. He insisted that all the team was family . . . he controlled it as a patriarchal figure."

In that spirit, Revie had ensured his players put away a proportion of their wages into a pension scheme. He also conducted a ritual massage every Thursday morning. And under Revie, a minister from Knaresborough would visit Elland Road for a weekly chat with the players. Revie's own attitude towards religion seems to have been ambiguous. He had begun his bed-time prayers (interruption of which had once so startled his old Sunderland team-mate Charlie Fleming) as a 12-year-old, looking for solace after his mother had died. More than 30 years later, Revie wrote in the *Evening Standard* that the England players should do the same, and "thank God they are doing something which they love and are being well paid for at the same time." Bob English, Revie's physiotherapist at Elland Road says: "Don always carried a little statue of St John inside his pocket everywhere he went. He was religious. I'm a Catholic and we used to talk about it."

When Revie told one journalist near the time of his death he was not religious, he may have meant that he had no theology. He was more of a fatalist, a believer in the luck of talismans, his make-up riddled with superstitions, some of which seemed almost more pagan than Christian. For what he may have prayed during his ritual night-time sessions, only Revie knew. Yet alongside all this ran his total belief in Sunday football, and for the most commercial reasons.

In Revie's personality, brooding uncertainty coexisted with conviction; the cares of the world mixed with light-heartedness.

"Don Revie had a great gift for keeping up morale. He could go round and see someone wasn't right, players, staff, anybody. We had bags of laughs, bags of giggles," Bob English says. Peter Lorimer recalls: "I used to love getting in the car and going down for training. The atmosphere was good and the boss had created this . . . a little fortress in which everyone was friendly and people appreciated everybody's play."

Lord Harewood was impressed by Revie's buoyant character. "He was absolutely serious and yet could laugh. I liked the way he could talk about plans. Once or twice we would go out on Saturday nights and get back in time to watch Match of the Day. It was great fun . . . and wonderful to watch it with him because he would see more than you or I could do. He had a rare ability to win people's confidence. I think the most impressive thing about Don was man management."

The charge of greed, laid so often before Revie, was not evident to those who knew him in his Leeds days. Had he been a full-time mercenary, it is unlikely he would have arrived at Elland Road with such modest personal finances. Peter Veitch says: "When he came to Leeds, he was a poor man. Don often used to say that after Manchester City won the FA Cup, there were no celebrations like there are today. His wage for that week was just £12. And he wasn't a wealthy man even when he left Leeds . . . they didn't pay him well. For what he'd done in the time he was there, he didn't leave with a lot of cash." For all that he bothered about their financial affairs, no Leeds player recalls any instance of Revie displaying personal avarice. But some who knew him in earlier years, including Raich Carter, Ken Barnes and his boyhood friend in Middlesbrough, George Tinsley, recall that money nagged away at his mind. While Revie enjoyed their juvenile gambling together, he had not been one to throw his money away.

Revie does not seem to have been born with the natural cunning of the grasper. Tinsley also recalls that as a boy the young Revie had to be given a lesson in the art of stealing chips from his father's wrapped lot, so that the theft might remain undetected between the fish shop and home. "Don would make a hole in the paper and pinch them. But his father wanted to know what had caused the holes. I said he should roll them out, take a few then roll then back again so that he couldn't find out," Tinsley says.

Revie became absorbed in money deals but not only on his own behalf. The contract with Admiral and another ill-fated venture with Austin Reed were for the benefit of the FA. He had increased bonuses for players. In approaching Bobby Robson as a possible successor at Leeds, after the directors rejected Johnny Giles, the flavour of their telephone exchange was as much about how Revie might help make Robson thousands more than if he remained with Ipswich Town. Revie's aims were often higher than making just himself financially secure. It was as if his mission was to do all he could for everyone connected with the precarious world of professional football. "He bent over backwards to help players make sure they got a fair deal," Mike Channon says. "He changed a lot of things and players are still benefitting. Even though you'd play for your country for nothing, he put England on a professional basis."

Yet this was the same Revie who had left Leeds secure with a lucrative ten-year consultancy deal but who, according to Syd Owen, had made no move to obtain contracts and a degree of security for his loyal lieutenants. The fabulous deal he had struck in the United Arab Emirates to escape his enemies in the England camp, the sleuths of the *Daily Mirror* or whoever, earned him scant sympathy. Seven years later, what might have been a return to English League management with Queen's Park Rangers foundered on his financial requirements. By that time, Revie's children had grown up and were making their way in the world, and any protest that his aim was to ensure his family's secure future would have rung hollow. At some stage, possibly as a reaction to his sense of having been underpaid for much of his stressful life, demanding more money than most people needed to live on comfortably seemed to become a habit with Revie.

Not that he lacked time for the sick or the needy. There are several instances of Revie directing his players to see children or the elderly in hospital. When he moved up to Scotland and before he was struck down with motor neurone disease, he became involved in various good causes. One who befriended him in that time is Jim Hossack, the Glasgow-based writer and broadcaster. "I first became involved with Don in staging a testimonial for George Young, the Scottish International footballer," says Hossack. "Don felt the fact he had never had a testimonial was a disgrace. He worked very, very hard. He would sell raffle tickets

. . . he would do anything for anybody. I never met a kinder man than Don Revie . . . he was one of the finest men I have met."

While Revie always had a sharp-eye for an opportunity in public relations, he also had time for people who were unimportant to the progress of his career. He could not have expected much kudos from developing relationships with individual supporters such as Dave Cox, a Leeds United fan who drove up regularly to Elland Road from Birmingham for home matches. Cox says: "I wrote to Don Revie to see if I could meet him one particular match. We exchanged letters and as the months progressed, he invited me up into the club lounge. About 20 times on match days, he found a quarter of an hour of his prime time to see me . . . say what was going on. He was a big man."

It would take a cynic to dismiss the reception given by Revie to one such loyal but relatively uninfluential fan as just another exercise in image enhancement. Mike Channon and Jeff Powell both agree: Don Revie wanted to be loved. That yearning may, as much as any public relations consideration, have lain behind the hospitality and apparent openness he displayed to the press. As England manager, the craving for public approval when he sensed many around him were hostile governed some of Revie's erratic team selections. It had all been so different at Leeds where he had been the godfather, his management firm, his visions clear, his control almost absolute.

Revie was one of the most serious football men ever. But how different his career might have been had he not fallen under the influence of Bill Sanderson, the manager of Middlesbrough Swifts, at such an impressionable age. As it was, Revie's head was full of strategies by the time he reached his early teens. Sanderson was the first of many footballing father-figures. There followed Septimus Smith and Johnny Duncan at Leicester City, and Raich Carter at Hull. Revie's enthusiasm at Manchester City for permutations of the plan that took his name was boundless, as his chapters in Soccer's Happy Wanderer reveal. By his mid-twenties he had a mature and clear vision of how football should be played.

An elegant and constructive player himself, Revie went on to preside over one of the meanest, and at times most negative, teams English League football had ever seen. It was the going rate for success at the time but continued success through battles of attrition was never Revie's ultimate aim. He intended that his team should flower – as it did – and that it should be loved, though it rarely was. Lord Harewood says: "I think he was rather romantic. Changing the strip to the all white of Real Madrid was a romantic thing to do and I think it worked . . . it was one of many signs that was good."

Joe Jordan, in common with several other Leeds players of the era believes that Revie might have achieved more had he allowed his players to blossom sooner. "The team was even better than the record showed . . . there should have been more belief in their ability. They should have been allowed to show their arrogance – in the right way – which they could have done. Leeds should have won more." Revie, of course, knew it too. Occasionally, he would jettison his caution such as before the 1972 Cup final against Arsenal when he told his team to "go out and play your own brand of beautiful football." Years later, when Eric Smith had taken over a League team in Cyprus that was suffering the tensions of a challenge for the League Championship, he telephoned his old friend Revie. "Don advised me to take the foot off the accelerator, ease up a bit and give them a bit of fun."

After the 1973 Cup final defeat Revie was, according to Jordan, so sick he was almost lost for words. Yet within a few months, his team was showing astounding powers of recovery, embarking on its miracle year with an unbeaten run of 29 matches that were played, for the most part, in terrific style. "In that year, it never entered my head we would be beaten," Jordan says. However much Revie lost, and by whatever foul methods he had sometimes achieved success, at other times he put out teams that played to near perfection.

The question asked of any English team claiming greatness, before or since, is: But were they as good as Leeds? When in 1987-88, Liverpool had a similar run of unbeaten matches before stumbling at the 30th hurdle, the media scrambled to compare them with Leeds. While Revie was increasingly immobilised by motor neurone disease, his great side, the side of a soccer visionary, was alive in everyone's memory once more. And were Liverpool as great? Few save their own supporters thought so. How many teams will leave such vivid memories as Revie's Leeds did with referee Jack Taylor? "They were a beautifully balanced side. If they had played in another country and you put different coloured shirts on them and blacked their faces, I would still know it was Leeds," he says.

The ghost of Don Revie has long haunted Elland Road. It may never be laid. Brian Clough felt it at every corner. He tried to exorcise it by, among other things, suggesting Revie's desk be taken away and burned. But instead, it was Clough who was to be driven out after just 44 days. There then followed as managers Jimmy Armfield, Jock Stein and Jimmy Adamson before a succession of Revie old boys, Allan Clarke, Eddie Gray assisted by Jimmy Lumsden, and then Billy Bremner assisted by Norman Hunter, were employed to revive Leeds United's fortunes. Although under Allan Clarke the club was to be relegated, no grudge was held against him by the Leeds supporters, for Clarke was a symbol of glories past, scorer of Leeds' only goal in their only FA Cup win. The fans had shown much more impatience towards his predecessor Jimmy Adamson, on whom they turned after a notably wretched goal-less home draw with Coventry in 1980. By that time, the Leeds fans had started looking back to the past and singing from the terraces "Bring back Don Revie to Leeds".

The succession of Revie old boys has been interpreted by some as a sign of the club's inability to break with its past, and a feeling that the directors were hoping Revie might somehow have transmitted some of his managerial genius to his protégés. It is something of a myth. The Leeds board in 1974 had sought to make a clean break with Revie, ignoring his suggestion that Johnny Giles should be the successor. There is not, nor ever has been, much sentimentality among the directors of Leeds United.

Terry Nash, chief executive of the club from 1983 to 1986, says: "There was no element of looking back. I had a feel for the processes that were going on. When Allan Clarke went, Eddie Gray had been injured and showed promise as a coach. He was a cheap but hopeful option . . . a thinking man. When Gray went and Bremner was recruited, it was a straightforward appointment. He had done well at Doncaster and was the opposite to Eddie Gray; less a thinking man, more a blood and guts chap. Though I suppose it had entered into consideration that Bremner and Gray were popular as players. Some of the directors had learned from the Brian Clough affair and were wary of big names."

The line of descent from Revie ended with the appointment of Howard Wilkinson as manager in 1988. Wilkinson, still conscious of the godfather's ghost, had a further purge of Revie memorabilia but retained a list of the honours achieved in his reign. Those, Wilkinson feels, are something that should be played up to. He has made a good start, leading Leeds out of the Second Division after eight years, bringing that championship to Elland Road for the first time since Revie won it in 1964.

Wilkinson has had to shoulder the burden of the history that Revie created; the fanatical expectation of success. Where many Leeds fans were once apathetic and almost timid, they became arrogant and bellicose, and smarted with a sense of indignity that their club should have been so long away from the big time. The hopes of supporters in the 1963-4 season were uncomplicated by comparisons with a great past. Leeds, with or without John Charles, had never belonged to the élite.

It will take more than the removal of mementoes and the burning of a desk to erase the ghost of Revie. Even an FA Cup or a Championship may not do it. For Wilkinson's players are just that: players, imported at a cost and on short contracts, though welded into a winning team with expertise. Revie's team were his sons and grew up alongside him: Sprake, Reaney, Cooper, Bremner, Charlton, Hunter, Lorimer, Clarke, Jones, Giles, Gray, Madeley, constantly giving their all for him, their names tripping off the tongue like some litany.

Peter Veitch says: "I don't think what happened at Elland Road could happen again. On their day, they were the best team in the world. It was really just two people, Don Revie and Harry Reynolds who got together and clicked. And it worked."

Many of that team played only for Revie. Joe Jordan, however, travelled more widely to Manchester United, AC Milan and Southampton but says: "He is the best manager I have been privileged to work under." Revie would have enjoyed hearing that, as he treasured many moments of his career. Yet overall, a sense of enjoyment is not associated with his memory. There was too much worry, too much acrimony, too many things lost that should have been won. Too rarely, perhaps, he gave vent to his true feelings. While the manner in which Leeds lost could move him to fury, Billy Bremner remains amazed by Revie's overall self-control. Or over-control, perhaps. "I can't be like him. How he bottled things up after a game until Monday, I'll never know," Bremner says.

"Show me a man who hasn't got any weaknesses. I'd like to meet him," Ted Croker says. "Don Revie had more strengths than weaknesses . . . he was a likeable man, a strong, down to earth man." This benign yet considered estimate comes from someone of whom Revie had once fallen foul. Yet except for an unyielding minority, Revie has come to be remembered less as a villain and more as a tragic figure.

In Revie's case the often-abused word "tragedy" is appropriate. He was an expansive, ambitious man, with more good in him than bad; one who achieved greatness and then fell into disgrace through the flaws in his character; and, in a fretful pursuit of success that might have come more readily if he could have trusted others or the course of nature, Revie may even have precipitated the savage disease that killed him. His life contained many of the classical elements of tragedy because of its scale, because of the extremes between rise and fall. And history, in which Revie's place is secure, is coming to judge him more kindly.